P. B. H. MAY

" Tall, good-looking, confident and accomplished . . ."

CRICKET
MY HAPPINESS

by

A. A. THOMSON

London 1956

THE SPORTSMANS
BOOK CLUB

To

Sir Pelham F. Warner,

that ' verray parfit gentil Knighte '

*This SBC edition was produced in 1956 for sale
to its members only by The Sportsmans Book Club. Full details are
obtainable from the proprietors, Phoenix House Ltd at 38 William IV
Street, Charing Cross, London WC2 and at Letchworth Garden City,
Hertfordshire. This edition is set in 11 pt Baskerville type leaded and
has been reprinted by Richard Clay & Co. Ltd at The Chaucer Press,
Bungay, Suffolk. It was first published by the Museum Press Ltd.*

INTRODUCTION

By C. B. FRY

As you know, the author of this consequently very welcome book not long ago produced another book called *Cricket My Pleasure*, which achieved an immediate and merited success with the *cognoscenti*—that is to say, it was much liked by readers who are good judges.

There is always the chance, and even the probability, that a book which is successful with the good judges will be a success with many more readers who, though they would not claim to be experts either in literary value or in special subject-matter, are nevertheless quite capable of being entertained.

Now it happens that when I was invited to supply a modest introduction I remembered that none other than the philosopher Aristotle (who has been a best-seller for over two thousand years) took some trouble to explain the difference between Pleasure and Happiness, the gist of his exposition being that though Pleasure is one of its components, Happiness is not at all the same content as Pleasure.

It occurs to me that anyone who is wise enough to read this present book, if he has not read the other, may very well catch up on Aristotle by doing so and forming his own opinion on the philosophical argument as to the relation of Pleasure and Happiness, which is really a question of considerable importance to all of us.

Meanwhile please note that when I asked our author what this new book is about, he replied that it has no special text except that *Cricket is for enjoyment and that cricketers understand it better than critics.*

If I may be critical myself, I beg to remark that our author should rather have said that Cricket ought to be for enjoyment and cricketers ought to understand it better than critics. And in support of the first limb of this correction may I point out that one chapter below is called " Cricket my Misery " and expounds that the game, like true love, has its moments of bliss, but is mostly agony; and, in support of the other limb, that almost the best judge of cricket I have ever known was Walter Buckmaster, who did not play cricket when at school with me nor, so far as I know, ever afterwards when he was the best polo-player in England and probably in the world. I would gladly have entrusted him singly to select the England eleven *v.* Australia and (if he would leave the Stock Exchange and his country home near Rugby) to manage our England team on any foreign tour. His knowledge of the game and of men was super-excellent.

So much in general; and to save words of commendation I herewith make a token wager that whoever reads the first two chapters of this book will read all the rest.

The other day I read in a book on cricket by an author who has popularized himself with some skill as well as merit that there are over four thousand books about or round about the game to be found in the British Museum catalogue. This reads to me a tall number; but if true, the statement adds a welcome to the four thousand and first and any others to come. But I will make a second token wager, to wit that none of its myriad predecessors is as ingenious as our present volume in discovering interesting novel topics on which to discourse. In short, I back our present author to hold his own against all comers, ancient and modern.

By the way, may I tell you how I judge a book on cricket? It is thus. I read the first chapter, and if I like it I read the last; then, if the book has an index, I look up my own name; and if I find it I read any paragraphs (or pages) about myself; then if I like what is said about me, or rather if I find it is judgmatic and true, I then peruse the whole book. This method saves a lot of time, or rather waste of time.

The last book I studied before this one was written by an old friend of mine who in his last chapter put me rather upon the horns of doubt.

Qua what he wrote. . . . He actually had the nerve to declare as follows: "Sport is older than civilization; and Homer, thousands of years ago, sang the praises of boxers in the Olympic Games at Athens, where all sorts of athletic contests took place every year."

This paragraph by my much-prized friend contains about as many slips as can be compressed into a paragraph. Sport came into being when people became civilized and wanted a replacement of the excitement and adventure they used to know in the olden days before civilization had obliterated war and the sheer necessity of hunting for food in forest and on hill-side with attendant danger. Sport was extended gradually to imitative adventure in field-games.

Homer lived at least not later than 800 B.C. The first Olympic Games were held as late as 776 B.C. or 774 B.C. and Pindar wrote of the Olympic Games, not Homer. The siege of Troy was ancient history when the Homeric poems were composed. I read the paragraph again and a light broke in. The whole thing was obviously ironical. Evidently my friend had noticed some fantastic errors in various recent books on cricket.

Why do I cite this? Because the man who made these slips is an experienced cricketer, a University graduate and a man of affairs who could only have slipped on purpose. And if he did this it may be worth your while to read carefully every word in *Cricket My Happiness* in order to catch the author out in some *gaffe* or other.

If you do you will be as pleased as I was to catch my old friend a-tripping.

But again in token I wager you will fail in this quest. At any rate I did.

It is a pleasure to meet with a book which at once delights the literary faculty and pleases the reader who knows the game.

C.B. Fry

CONTENTS

A 2

ILLUSTRATIONS

CHAPTER I

THE OVAL BALCONY

I

Whatever the hanging committee of the Royal Academy may say, for me the picture of the year was that of Len Hutton smiling the smile of victory from the balcony at the Oval on the 19th of August 1953. A handsome victory, a handsome smile, a handsome captain. He had been run out the evening before, by one of those disasters which showed the fallibility of the infallible, and on this fourth afternoon he could take no more part in the game with his body, though everybody knew where his heart and soul were. In that picture he is not in cricketing flannels, but his jacket is off, and the rest of his 'civilian' clothes show their usual new-pin neatness. In his right hand is a cigarette, symbol of relaxation; his left hand is raised in friendly greeting towards his thirty thousand admirers surging over the turf below. His expression is that of a captain who has steered his ship home into harbour and does not now mind how rough the passage has been. His look is serene. He is a man who need not even bother to laugh at his critics. The facts did that for him.

There he stood, on the balcony, the architect of victory as surely as Trevor Bailey had been its most honourable and monumental bricklayer: England's first professional captain since the ancient days of Lillywhite, Alfred Shaw and Shrewsbury. Yes, a professional had captained England and led his country to glorious victory. But I do not believe for one instant that Lord Hawke was turning in his grave. In the golden pavilion of the Elysian Fields they understand these matters a good deal better than they did when they were here. . . . As a captain Hutton succeeded through intelligent forethought and by the quiet winning of loyalty among the eleven who were also his friends. I do not think he ever had any

Fuehrer-like intuitions. He worked out a plan and held steadfastly to it. Many people talk piously about the virtues of team work: it takes leadership of a high quality to achieve and mould it. In times of doubt and difficulty he won, and kept, unshakable loyalty. Earlier in the series he had been subjected to a certain amount of abuse: some of it from the bottomlessly ignorant and some—slightly dastardly stuff—from critics who should have known better, but he treated it all with a decency and dignity that Lord Hawke could not but have admired.

The population of the United Kingdom at the last census was about fifty million, and very few of these seem to have refrained from writing a book on the 1953 Tests, particularly on the last one. All that need be set down here is a record of one person's hopes and fears and final happiness during those five paralysing days. I had seen two days of the Lord's match, and as there is a limit to annual leave, even during the year of an Australian visit, I had only one day's leave left and no ticket. I had beforehand to choose one day out of the three, four, five, or possibly six or seven, for the privilege of getting up at five o'clock and standing, semi-conscious and more than semi-anxious, outside the Oval from the grey dawn onwards. The first day seemed safe enough to tackle from a distance. It was Saturday and I could listen at home all the afternoon. Monday might be more exciting or more terrifying. Better wait till then.

As soon as I reached home, I rushed to the radio. It is an ordinary 'steam' set; I do not possess a television receiver; that I must leave to my half-a-crown-a-week tenants, and good luck to them. I was, however, nobly served by the 'sound' commentators, who appear to toil for my especial pleasure. Their matter is what the gods send them, but their manner, in its varied ways, is superb. It is a melancholy fact that one never learns to listen patiently and rationally. When I first switched on, the Australian score was 98 for two, and how did anybody expect a man to have any lunch when he heard that Hassett and Harvey were holding their own without apparent trouble and that it was raining, anyway? One took the fact that Hutton had lost the toss as a matter of course; by the fifth time it had become almost a law of nature. At least play was starting again. Australia, it seemed, were on the point of settling down when Hassett was suddenly snapped at the wicket, without addition to the score. Harvey was out to a running catch by Hutton, judged to a hair and beautifully taken. The listener, I say, is irrational. When no wickets fall, he is outraged. When one falls, he wants another. When two fall, he feels like a tiger that has tasted blood, and wants a collapse. I was quite irritated that the next wicket did not fall till 118, and then there was quite a stand before the sixth fell at 160. The seventh wicket, too, gave the bowlers (and myself) no trouble at all, and the outlook seemed to be set fair. This was undoubtedly the stuff to give them. This was listeners' paradise. Then Lindwall went in and batted with all those qualities of courage, resolution and the offensive spirit which are extolled in the official citations for gallantry. Posthumous decorations have been awarded for less. The score mounted. It was for me the beginning of a long-drawn agony.

When a man speaks of the frailty of human nature, he is usually seeking excuses for his own degrading conduct. At this distance of time, and with the Ashes safely won, I can see Lindwall's innings for what it was: a brave act of defiance. In the same way, too, I can now look objectively on Langley's bold 18 and even on Johnston's outrageous 9 not out. There used in my young days to be but seven wonders of the world, but where would you place Bill Johnston's batting average? It is the sort of thing Victorian families used to have stuffed. But, while it lasted, it slew me. I was no gentleman, no sportsman. I was a mere disembodied emotion, demanding irrationally and unjustly of the gods: " How *can* our bowlers hurl the seven best batsmen out for a song and then let these tail-end charlies get away with murder? " Unfair, I agree. But to see those runs piling up was almost unbearable. I ought to have shown more gratitude to Evans and Edrich for the fine catches that dismissed Lindwall and Langley. I ought to have paid tribute to Trueman's 4 for 86, vindication of a fine lad's north-country doggedness and perseverance; I ought to have gone on my knees to thank heaven, fasting, for a good man's bowling and Bedser's record number of wickets—39—in a Test series. As it was, I merely felt that 275 was a larger score than the enemy were entitled to. When, in the last darkling overs of the day, Hutton's cap (the cap in which he had on the same ground in 1938 made 364) fell off as he jumped to kill a fast-rising ball, and almost dropped on his stumps, I suspected that my heart would never function evenly again.

Sunday, the nominal day of rest, intervened to soothe the harrowed nerves. In the morning I met two of the Australian players and wished them all the luck in the world except in one thing. " Too right," said they in effect; " we knew you would. . . ." Monday played itself in hopefully. Edrich batted well. May played an innings as valuable as many an easier century, and Hutton, as ever, carried his country's fortunes on Atlas-shoulders. Then England, as England had done on Saturday, allowed a firm advantage to slip away. From 137 for one the score dribbled away, as though through some invisible leak, to 210 for six and 225 for seven. Once more England owed survival to Bailey, the Knight of the Brick Wall, and how England could have lived without Bailey I tremble to think. . . .

Tuesday was the day. Can you imagine me (or even a genuinely conscientious person) sitting quietly in an office with the world rocking outside and depending on pure chance for news of triumph or disaster? Bailey was the major hero, as he had been at least three times before in the series. Trueman was half a hero and Bedser three-quarters. The crowd went into transports of joy as England slipped in front, and when the innings ended with a lead of 31, each one of those runs seemed of pure gold.

But the rapture was to come. Word came to me from a colleague at the far end of my building who, in turn, was receiving signals from some honest workmen who had a television set in a factory on the opposite side of the road. The progress of the battle was conveyed to me by telephone—an instrument I had not previously admired—and though it started sedately, the tempo of the match perceptibly quickened. There is nothing to affect the blood pressure in a score of 59 for one, but . . . the telephone rang.

" Hello? "

" Fifty-nine for two. It's Hole."

Pause and ping.

" Hello? Who is it? "

" Sixty for three. It's Harvey."

" Hello? Who is it? "

" Sixty-one for four. It's Miller."

Short pause and ping-ping.

" Hello? Who is it now? "

" Sixty-one for five. Now it's Morris. They're on the run."

The thing was incredible, outside and beyond human possibility. Sixty-one for five. Hassett, Hole, Harvey, Miller and Morris had travelled the broad road. *We have them.* These wickets had fallen so unbelievably quickly that I could no longer exercise normal patience. Five minutes passed. Nothing happened. Ten minutes. The telephone bell rang shrilly and I snatched the receiver with shaking hand.

" Who is it now? "

" The Foreign Office," replied a slightly outraged voice, " if you have no objection."

The next time the telephone rang I asked a colleague with stronger nerves than mine to answer it. Now that time has passed and I am comparatively sober, I like to think that I should have enjoyed that innings of Archer's if I had seen it. It was an effort of the utmost valour. He will live to make many centuries, but never a century better than that 49. But I doubt if I should have appreciated the sight of it at that moment, valiant as it was. It would have seemed to me that, for the third time in that match, England was letting the chance of victory slip. Happily, not quite. The telephone rang again. . . .

" It's someone who says that a Mr. Davidson has gone. Rather mysterious. Would you like to speak to him? "

" No, thanks. So long as Mr. Davidson's gone . . ."

And, of course, the innings ended for 162 and the Ashes were only 132 runs away. It was a personal tragedy for a great and good man, when Hutton was run out for no reason at all. But, in spite of this, confident hope survived the evening.

My daughter and I were at the Oval early in the morning. It is not my favourite ground, so far as the amenities go, but it must have seen more exciting Test finishes than any other: 1882, 1902, 1912, 1926, and now this. After our long wait, we sat on the edge of the grass and watched Edrich and May defend with determination and steely nerve. What was wholly magnificent was the way the Australians in the field fought every run: Harvey, Davidson, Archer, Hole, what electrifying fielders these young men are. . . . The bowling was good, but the fielding was little short of miraculous. Runs came slowly, but there was no hurry. Half an hour before lunch May was out. It did not matter. He had acquitted himself manfully. Nobody could doubt that he had won his spurs. It was nearly three o'clock when the end came. Edrich, amid well-merited cheers, reached his fifty and then Compton, with a lusty crack, made the winning hit. Laughing and shouting we ran across the grass.

" We want Len. We want Len. *We want Len !* "

Out he came, went in again, and then came out with the rest of the English team. Out came Hassett, too. When Hutton spoke, he spoke modestly, as always, and I knew that his moment of personal triumph, which he was the first to share with his team-mates, would give delight to many thousands all over Britain's (and cricket's) Commonwealth, to his Yorkshire admirers—what is the population of the county, anyway?—to his county captain and co-selector, the unselfish Norman Yardley, to his mentor, Herbert Sutcliffe, who confidently asserted twenty years ago that this would happen, and to a frail old gentleman with a golden heart named George Hirst, who knows that his eighty-odd years have been well worth living. . . .

The next day I spoke to my very important superior and

apologized for what I euphemistically called my wandering attention of Tuesday.

"Think nothing of it, my boy," he said kindly. "You should have seen 'em in the House of Lords. . . ."

2

It was when we were tearing across the Oval turf that my daughter should have said to me: "And now, Daddy, tell me about 1926. . . ." But she did not. The young never ask the right questions. My only consolation lies in the certainty that their grandchildren will undoubtedly say: "Oh, lord, Grandpa's away about Hutton and Bedser again. . . ."

The 1926 Oval game, of which I was lucky enough to see two days, came at the end of a series which had up to that time produced some tall scoring, the usual weather at Manchester and four draws. The fifth game, at the Oval, was due to be played to a finish, and, as so often happens in these circumstances, it never looked like not being finished. England put a finely blended team into the field, though it looked rather different from the one that had sported some weeks before in the usual rain at Manchester. George Geary and Larwood came in and Rhodes came back, in place of Ernest Tyldesley, Kilner and Root. A. P. F. Chapman, who then seemed to me the young darling of the gods, took over the captaincy from the plucky but unlucky A. W. Carr. Sir Pelham Warner has described one dramatic point of dialogue at the final meeting of selectors: Warner, Perrin and Arthur Gilligan, with Hobbs and Rhodes as co-opted members.

"Can you still pitch a length, Wilfred?"

"Oh, well, I can keep 'em there or thereabouts."

Chapman, who was a lucky captain and richly deserved to be, won the toss, and Hobbs and Sutcliffe started off in their usual masterly fashion. The 50 went up in an hour and, just as the spectators were settling back to enjoy another of those polished hundred partnerships, Mailey bowled Hobbs with a full toss. What was said by Hobbs, most courteous and controlled of all players, is not generally known, but Mailey is reported to have

exclaimed: " Well, I never ! " Then followed a series of evil
events which a tolerant critic described as due to an un-
accountable display of reckless batting. On paper that batting
order looked as invulnerable as the Bank of England, but cracks
began to show. . . . Woolley mistimed a googly and Hendren,
that inveterate puller, dragged an off-ball on to his stumps.
Chapman, new captain and happy young warrior, set about
knocking Mailey to glory and had almost succeeded in this
praiseworthy object when Oldfield stumped him. Stevens
went next and then the immovable Sutcliffe at the other end
was removed by what I can only describe as evil chance. I did
not see the ball which rose from his pads and hit him a boxer's
blow on the end of the nose but I did see, two days later, a whole
succession of balls which hit and bruised him all over the body.
To call him an iron man would have been paying a compliment
to a baser metal. After that bang on the nose, the next ball
looped the loop and bowled him. It was left to Tate and
Rhodes to pull the innings back into shape again, and this they
did with strong determination. Even so, a score of 280 was no
adequate total for a timeless contest on a pretty good wicket.
Before the day's end the English bowlers had begun to redeem
the side's comparative batting failures. Bardsley was snatched
by Strudwick at the wicket. Macartney, who was attempting
a knock-'em-off-their-length act, similar to Chapman's, was
bowled by an atrocious bouncer; Ponsford was run out and
Andrews had his off-stump sent cart-wheeling. Four for 60
sent the crowd home happy.

The next day Woodfull fell early to one of the best balls even
Rhodes ever sent down. It was Collins—' Horse-shoe ' to his
friends—who paved the hard way to Australian recovery, but it
was Gregory, after Arthur Richardson had been beautifully
caught by Geary, who swung the game right round by hitting
hard, high and often. Then there was a further fighting rear-
guard action by Oldfield, who was always a finer bat than a
wicket-keeper of his quality needed to be, and Grimmett, who
was not a master-batsman, but made 35 priceless runs just the
same. The Australians finished 22 runs in front and England's

grip on the game had slipped. There was an hour to play, and Hobbs and Sutcliffe played it out serenely, as though the bowling were easy and the game of no great importance. Forty-nine for none. If either of them had lost his wicket that evening, cricket history would have been different and poorer. But the pillars of Hercules stood firm.

I was at the Oval incredibly early the next morning. There had been a battering thunderstorm the night before but there was now no more rain, only scudding clouds and fitful, steamy sunshine. As long as good men gather in wet pavilions, they will always argue about what was the best innings ever played. There can be few living who saw Charles Bannerman's 165 (retired hurt) out of 245 at Melbourne in 1877, and the number of people who saw Prince Ranjitsinhji's 154 not out at Manchester in 1896 or Jessop's century plus four at the Oval in 1902 must grow smaller every year. Jessop's century, plus J. T. Tyldesley's 63 in 1904 on Melbourne's notorious glue-pot, when nobody else, except Trumper on the other side, made more than a trifle: these are the two brightest efforts within my conscious lifetime, but of those I have actually seen, Sutcliffe's on that 17th of August 1926 was, with one possible exception, the most valiant. And Hobbs's was the next best. Those two defied the world and put on 112 before lunch. If either of them had faltered, the dyke would have been fatally breached. Hobbs was bowled by a bail-kisser soon after lunch. He had made exactly a hundred, and if even he ever made a better, I should like to know which of his 197 hundreds it was. Three lively but not lengthy stands followed: Woolley and Sutcliffe, Hendren and Sutcliffe, and Stevens and Sutcliffe. As in the first innings, Sutcliffe never looked like getting out, though he often looked like getting maimed. Early on he had received so many blows that he might have been knocked unconscious, but he gave out the impression to the world that, as long as he was conscious, nothing could shift him. Suddenly eternity ended. With almost the last ball of the day Mailey shifted him. For a moment the crowd was absolutely silent and then, as Sutcliffe moved towards the pavilion, limping but still defiant, the roar rose and swelled. He had made 161 and every single run was worth a fortune. With the passing of the years, I can see Mailey's point of view, too, though naturally such broad-mindedness was not granted to me then. Along with Gregory, Grimmett, Macartney and Richardson, he had toiled all day and taken punishment like a galley-slave. The sight of Sut-cliffe's back must have seemed the fairest prospect he had viewed for many a day. When England went to bed that night they had put on 331 and still had four wickets to fall and I devoutly prayed that Sutcliffe and Hobbs would sleep peace-fully, if only they could find a large enough unbruised area on their respective anatomies to lie on.

I was at the Oval even earlier the following day, and the hour at which I had to leave my home in rural Essex to do so is just nobody's business. I remember as I write the cramp that gripped my legs from sitting inside the rails. I even remember the wrinkles in the neck, like canals on Mars, of the Surrey supporter who sat, equally cramped, in front of me. We had one fright before play started. There was a sudden sharp shower and we had to sit, getting wet, in, and on, our cramped quarters because there was nowhere to go without losing our places. It was a short shower, followed by a ration of watery sunshine. There was much speculation as to whether play would start at the proper time. My Surrey friend was prepared to make a demonstration in the event of a delay, but he simmered down when he saw Collins leading his men out. Geary was soon caught at the wicket, but after that there was a useful stand between Rhodes and Tate. The Sussex man enjoyed himself hugely, always setting out with humorous hope-fulness for the extra run and grinning all over his jolly face when Rhodes, a basically serious character, showed himself to be more cautious. Together they put on 43 excellent runs, and when the innings ended at 436, Tate was 33 not out.

It rained again in the lunch hour and we sheltered under an inadequate bivouac of newspapers. The players came out about an hour late. Cramped as we were, and steaming mildly after the second of our heavy showers, we were optimistic. But it was impossible to conceive an optimism as golden as the facts were beginning to warrant. Woodfull, the unbeatable, was the first to go. Early in Larwood's first over he half-cut a streaky one behind the wicket and Chapman signalled Geary up to third slip. Off the very next ball Geary took the first of his two lovely catches and there was only one run on the board. Macartney came out next, a man incapable of dullness; the score mounted to 31 and then an exceptionally swift and lifting ball from Larwood touched the edge of Macartney's bat and shot spinning venomously into the hands of Geary, who held it, amid rapturous applause, a beauty-queen among catches. Then came the procession. Ponsford was taken almost on the ground by Larwood off Rhodes, another fine catch. Collins came next, gaining a long greeting of applause for a sporting captain and a friendly foe as he strode to the wicket. He had made only 4 when Woolley accepted the fourth slip catch of the innings. It was one of those days when the English fieldsmen could do no wrong, for the next Australian, Andrews, after a hard hit or two, drove with all his strength at a shorter ball from Larwood, and was astonished to see it remain in Tate's outstretched right hand. Perhaps Tate was astonished, too. Bardsley at the other end had been solidly and stolidly holding the fort, but now his turn came to go. He had made 21 in stubborn fashion, but now he gave Woolley a simple catch, and Woolley did not drop simple catches. Each time a wicket fell the cheers of the crowd became more joyful and incredulous. It was wonderful; but surely, my native northern caution suggested, it could not be. Woodfull, the mighty Macartney, Ponsford, Andrews and Collins had gone, and now Bardsley the obstinate had gone, too. Surely, I felt, I was bound to open my eyes and discover that I had dreamt these miracles. Another roar. Gregory, that bonnie fighter of the first innings, made a wild slash at a ball from Tate, who had come on instead of Larwood, and Sutcliffe did not let a great fielding side down. Still another roar. This bade farewell to Richardson, who, after scratching four, was beaten, baffled and bewildered by a ball from Rhodes which did practically everything but say How Do. The score was 87 for eight. It was, of course, impossible. When, twenty years later, on the same ground, the Australians were 61 for five, it was also impossible. But, for the record, it happened to be true.

There was one final half-hour of sharp resistance from those tough resisters, Oldfield and Grimmett. Their stand put on 27 and the crowd became quite irrationally impatient. But Oldfield was eventually bowled by Stevens—every England bowler took at least one wicket—and then, while the clock pointed to five minutes past six, Geary bowled Mailey, a grand googly bowler and an able cartoonist but not at this moment the batsman to stand between England and her destiny. The instant he was out, Mailey dropped his bat and grabbed the ball as a souvenir, narrowly beating Strudwick, who had to settle for a stump. This was the victory that England had waited for since 1912. The team, under its gay young captain, had batted well and, especially in that fourth innings, bowled and fielded flawlessly. Hobbs and Sutcliffe had played like the proud masters they were. Rhodes, in his forty-ninth year, had placed the coping stone on his mighty Test career, while a young man named Harold Larwood, twenty-seven years his junior, had laid the foundation stone of his.

We tore across the turf and stood in front of the balcony, shouting and clapping. We yelled for Chapman. He came out, with a smile that was half a schoolboy's and half a cherub's. We went on yelling: for Hobbs, for Sutcliffe, and for Rhodes, especially Rhodes. When he came out, and he was a long time in coming, he looked in front of him as if there were nobody there. Finally, he smiled, the slightly grim smile of a conqueror who would have made an even more efficient job of it if he had been allowed by his fellow generals to get at the enemy sooner. The crowd, just as it did twenty-seven years later, was enjoying a moment of magnificent release. It had waited fourteen years for victory and this, it judged, was the moment when care could be cast aside, hats thrown in the air, and the thing humorously called by the foreigner ' English reserve ' torn to shreds and jumped on. Australians, who are brought up to think of the English as something in the nature of stuffed citizens, are surprised on the occasions when the English let themselves go. This happens, so far as my experience goes, only at a Coronation or when England wins a rubber at the Oval. Now we do not want another Coronation for at least sixty years, but the other matter is easier. All we have to do is beat the Australians more often.

3

Going back still further on our time machine, we may turn from the pleasing sight of Len Hutton's victorious and happy smile in 1953 and from A. P. F. Chapman's broader grin in 1926. Before that, though we do not have to go back so far in actual years, we have to go back to a different world. It is not so much a matter of time as of eternity, for England's previous home victory in a rubber against the Australians was in 1912. And who was the English captain who then came out and graciously smiled from the balcony? Wait till I tell you.

An interesting year, 1912. At least, it was to me, because it was the first time I had visited London, that wicked city; an interesting year for many thousands of my fellow-citizens, too, because it was the wettest year since Noah. Indeed, if that maritime character had had to play on some of the pitches endured by English, Australian and South African cricketers in 1912, he might have taken to drink sooner than he did, or have stayed in the pavilion on Mount Ararat until the following season.

Imagine me, then an incredibly callow north-country lad, gaping round London for the first time. I had come from my West Riding home town to King's Cross in a train which performed in exactly four hours the same journey which today, owing to progress and the rush and hurry of modern life, takes nearer six. I knew what I wanted to see: Madame Tussaud's, recently graced by the presence of a distinguished new-comer, one Dr. Crippen, and the House of Commons, where from the Gallery I heard Opposition back-benchers, far worse-mannered than the rather polite and colourless members of today, barracking the Prime Minister and the First Lord of the Admiralty, that subversive young Radical, Winston Churchill. I had also (virtually for the first time) visited a theatre where I witnessed a performance of *Macbeth*, every word of which was audible at the back of the gallery. We have now changed all that, of course, and audibility is stigmatized by the sophisticated as ham. Nevertheless I look back on that possibly corny performance as a landmark in my life and reflect that only God can make a Tree.

Lord's was on my list, of course, but that historic monument to my fellow-Yorkshireman was for a long time a disappointment, for every time I looked at a bus labelled St. John's Wood it started to rain. Lord's in 1912 was as wet as Old Trafford in any year within Manchester's memory. It was the year of the Triangular Tournament, the only one in history. Some people will tell you that the experiment was a dismal failure, as if there were something essentially miserable about triangularity for its own sake; whereas the truth is that every prospect pleased us and only the weather was vile. As for the cricketers, England were pretty good; South Africa were not very good; and Australia were hardly as good as they might have been. But they were not so bad, either. Because of unhappy quarrels at home, they landed on these shores without Trumper or Clem Hill, but they brought the mighty atom, Macartney, an almost unshiftable left-hander, Bardsley, and a deceptively destructive fast-medium bowler, Hazlitt. They also brought a diminutive leg-spinner named T. J. Matthews, who was to appear even more remarkable than Hazlitt. In one of the Tests against the South Africans he did the hat trick twice: once in each innings. Neither of these extraordinary bowlers did anything very extraordinary afterwards.

Each of the sides played the other two on three occasions. England beat the South Africans three times and Australia beat them twice. England and Australia fought, not so much against each other, as against weeping skies. At Lord's, England had a fine first innings, including a beautifully built century by Hobbs; Australia also had a fine first innings, including an even more glittering near-century by Macartney. Then it rained. At Manchester England had an innings in which only Rhodes (92) made more than 20, and about this game my step-Uncle Walter said: " They weren't *laking*, they were paddling." It was an arithmetical progression in the wrong direction. The victims started play at 3 p.m. on the first day, at 5 p.m. on the second, and on the third they never got around to starting at all.

The Oval match, which I attended (along with 30,000 other people), was scheduled by agreement to be played to a finish, or, at any rate, to last six days. The first two matches having been drawn owing to rain, this seemed the most sensible way of obtaining a finish. At first the weather looked like winning, as in the first two games, and in the end it took four days, between showers, a long time for an English Test in those days, before the weather was finally defeated. After two world wars, a series of economic depressions and a long rationing period during which the best Wensleydale cheese was practically unobtainable; after these terrible hardships, I say, the British race has learnt to possess its soul in patience. In 1912 people were not so meek. In any event psychologists had not yet invented the word ' frustration ' as an excuse for all human misconduct. We were frustrated all right. As we sat on those wooden benches which even the most loyal Surrey supporters could not have called comforting, and as we watched the sun shining down in mockery, it was hard for 30,000 impatient souls to realize that the wicket was not fit to play on. The pitch was, in fact, practically a quaking bog. Human nature being what it is, however, the average spectator grows indignant if the players do not bound into the arena to entertain him the instant the rain stops. When they did not come out, the crowd grew restive. At intervals certain discouraging characters, probably unemployed funeral-mutes, slow-marched sombrely round the ground bearing notice-boards covered with pessimistic prophecies about the start of play.

Rumour flashed round the ground—I don't know whence it emanated—that Gregory, the Australian captain, wanted to start but that Fry, the English captain, did not. Each, it was said, wanted to manoeuvre the other out on to this wicket which the sun was rapidly turning into something worse than a twenty-two-yard fly-paper. Eventually we heard that Fry had won the toss and in spite of all temptations to do something clever, he sent Hobbs and Rhodes out to bat. The winter before, these two had broken many records (and Australian bowlers' hearts), and they proceeded methodically with their foundation-laying task. Hobbs was the best batsman in the world (except Trumper), and Trumper, alas for Australia, was not there. Rhodes, that semi-miraculous figure who had shot up the batting ladder from No. 11 to No. 2, was Hobbs's perfect partner; not even Hobbs and Sutcliffe ran more understandingly between wickets than Hobbs and Rhodes. Hobbs in 1912 was as much a supreme master on that treacherous turf as he was to be fourteen years later. Probably he was the greatest batsman on an evil wicket that cricket ever saw (again, except Trumper or maybe Johnnie Tyldesley). Rhodes's defence was as immovable as the Pennines; indeed, it had a true Pennine quality. Between them they put up the hundred —what other human beings could have raised fifty?—and then Carkeek, the South Australian stumper with the queer name, grabbed Hobbs at the wicket. The elegant Spooner fell to an impossible catch by Hazlitt's out-stretched right hand which defied the conventional laws of gravity and which Macartney said afterwards was the best catch ever taken by mortal man. It may be so. I did not see George Ulyett catch Bonnor in 1886, and so I cannot say.

Then came Fry, at his own position of No. 4, and the crowd started to boo him as the reputed villain who had delayed, for some sinister reason, the start of the game, and robbed honest Londoners of their money's worth. It was a moment of moral crisis in my young life. Booing on a cricket-field is one of the nastiest of sounds. I had my private view of this man, Fry, the miscreant who had piled up so many sinful hundreds against Yorkshire A lad was not called on to love his enemies beyond a certain extent. But this was different. A party man, be he never so fervent, must join a wartime coalition. To hoot England's captain in the face of the common foe (and on a sticky wicket) was black treason. I clapped him till my palms were sore, and, when my neighbours scowled at me, I clapped all the harder. Thus encouraged, he scored only half a dozen runs in forty-five minutes. Rhodes missed his fifty by one, and then it was tea-time.

It is a cheering thought merely to recall that batting side. There were useful knocks from the stubborn J. W. H. T. Douglas and F. R. Foster, who, with Barnes, had formed England's two-handed engine of destruction in Australia the winter before. And there was a 60-odd from Frank Woolley that sparkled like diamonds and was worth its weight in them. The total of 245 was as respectable as could have been hoped for on such a wicket.

The enemy started sensationally and the crowd roared when Barnes sent back Syd Gregory for a single and clean bowled the mercurial Macartney for four. To do that you had to be the best bowler in the world. Barnes was. Then Bardsley, notably an obstinate character, joined Kelleway, one of nature's diggers in, and dug in. When rain finally stopped play—it had held it up several times before—they had fought their way step by step to 51 for two.

The next day's play consisted of an hour and a half, but rarely can an hour and a half have been more tightly packed. The Australian pair began bravely again in the morning and, patient as bricklayers, they built their score up to 90. By then a fiery sun had completed its fell work of drying out the wicket. Woolley and Barnes did the rest. Before 20 runs had been added, the rest of the Australians had walked to the middle and back again. It was for them a sad pilgrimage but we, the spectators, gloried in their sorrows.

But rain (and the inconvenient sunshine that alternated with it) fell alike on the just and on the unjust. When England went in again, Nature did not suddenly begin to smile. A tall bowler named Whitty found a hole in Rhodes's solid bat, and Wilfred went for 5. Spooner, the ' best-looking ' batsman between Palairet and Hammond, was pocketed—almost frisked —in the slips first ball. I doubt if ever another batsman of genius was unlucky enough to be dismissed twice in one match by catches which were out of this world. Life is essentially unjust. When Fry came in, the crowd hooted him once more. Their enmity seemed to me as motiveless as Iago's. They may have been suffering from a guilt complex and were subconsciously worrying about what would happen next, but, of course, we were not all psychiatrists then. Fry was a man against the world. He survived first the hat-trick, and then half a dozen overs of the utmost venom. It was a triumph of character over aggressive bowling, a wicked wicket and a hostile crowd. Even Hobbs, at the other end, could not score with ease and, when he attempted violence with a view to destroying the bowlers' dominance, was caught at point for 32. Woolley, seldom a failure, failed. The sky darkened like Judgment Day. When the downpour sent the players scurrying in an hour before their proper time, the evening and the morning were the third day, and England were 64 for four.

I have asked it before and may well ask it again: which was the best fighting Test innings the Oval gasometers—I refuse to call them gas-holders—have ever seen? Jessop's in 1902? Sutcliffe's in 1926? Hutton's in 1938 or 1950? I might conceivably vote for Sutcliffe, but nothing will convince me that C. B. Fry's in 1912 was not among the greatest. The wicket in the morning was a slough, a swamp. Young Jack Hearne gave him some useful help, and Douglas, always a sticker, stuck with him till lunch time. The sky was as unfriendly as the bowling. In the early afternoon Fry and Douglas defended the stockade, until the board read 170 for five. In his career Fry made ninety-four centuries, but I doubt if any one of them had quite the high quality of his 79 that day.

Then came the fantastic episode of Hazlitt, a fastish-medium bowler with a queer action. It was said that he could make the ball 'flutter'. . . . He undoubtedly fluttered English hearts that day. He had Douglas leg-before-wicket and Fry was taken in the slips. (He said afterwards that the divot his last stroke hacked out of the ground was bigger than the ball the fieldsman caught.) The thing went on like a massacre. Hazlitt took seven wickets for 25, the last five for one run. The crowd had become silent. If England had not been in such peril, I should have said that it served the spectators right for hooting England's captain. The score had been 170 for five, now it was 175 all out. Foster carried out his bat for three. It was almost a gallant effort. . . .

So Australia were left to make 310 to win, and in that dark period of anti-climax they never looked like getting them. Before a run had been scored, the provident Kelleway hit a ball from Dean deep and square on the off. Douglas caught it, dropped it, caught it, dropped it, practically playing a whole movement of Ravel's Bolero with the ball against his chest. I do not now suppose that this Cinquevalli stuff actually went on for ten minutes, but that is what it seemed like to me at the time. When I opened my eyes, Kelleway was taking his reluctant departure.

The great Macartney, partnered by a lively fellow named Jennings, hit out as if he meant to knock off the 300-odd runs before finally darkness fell. Nobody had a right to treat Barnes with such disrespect, and his captain asked him to change over, giving way to Woolley. But the break came at the other end, where, with the fifty in sight, Dean bowled Macartney. Without another run on the board Bardsley was run out; some madness must have entered into him, for only a man of marked suicidal tendencies would have attempted a short run with Jack Hobbs at cover. The run-stealers could not flicker to and fro to any great extent when Hobbs was on sentry-go. After that, the innings rapidly declined and fell. Dean and Woolley, Woolley and Dean: Woolley with his graceful action and his long left arm swinging right behind his body; Dean, a typical Lancashire man, ruddy, quizzical and humorous, with a heavy, lumbering run. He had a knack of being fastish on a good wicket and fraudulently slow on a bad one. This was a bad one, one of the worst ever. The next highest stand after Macartney's exit was *eleven*, rather painfully compiled by Jennings and Hazlitt for the ninth wicket. At last Jennings made a tremendous mishit which went up and, for some appreciable time, appeared reluctant to come down. Fry called, in turn, on Smith, the stumper, on Rhodes and (for some unexplained psychological reason) on George Hirst, who, to the best of my knowledge, was in Huddersfield at the time. Then Fry, suddenly running in from nowhere to nowhere, took the catch, one-handed, a few inches above the ground. Australia were all out for 65 and England had won by 244. This was the first of the three times in which I have run across the Oval turf to cheer England's captain. Fry, Chapman, Hutton. . . . Each one of them was a fine captain for me.

The fickle crowd went milling across the ground towards the pavilion and shouted for the captain to come out on the balcony to acknowledge their plaudits. Fry, however, took the view that the right time for plaudits was not now, but when he had been fighting for England's life at the beginning of his second innings. He would not come out, and I, for one, did not blame him. A large proportion of the other 29,999 did. I have since learned that a highly characteristic bit of dialogue took place immediately afterwards.

" Now, Charles," said Ranji, who was in the dressing-room, " be your noble self."

And Fry replied: " This is not one of my noble days."

But if Fry's 79 was not a noble innings, I have never seen one, before or since.

The oddest thing about this fine game is that, but for Hazlitt's fabulous spell of bowling, England could not have won. If it had not been for his fantastic taking of five wickets for one run, England would have gone on comfortably piling up a decent score, and there would have been no time to get Australia out that day. Ten minutes after play ended, the rain

VICTORY AT THE OVAL

" For me the picture of the year was that of Len Hutton smiling the smile of victory from the balcony at the Oval . . ."

W. S. SURRIDGE AND G. A. R. LOCK

" Catches seem to go to him as smaller fish go into the mouth of a giant pike . . ."

came down and did not stop, to the best of my recollection, for about fifty-six hours.

That evening, just to make life perfect, I saw Marie Lloyd and Harry Lauder for a shilling. The thought crossed my mind that if I could have had C. B. Fry up there in the gallery, I should indeed have been among the gods.

CHAPTER II

HAPPY JACK, HAPPY JOHNNY

I

ONE of the most charming books of its kind that has ever come my way is *The Happy Cricketer* by ' Country Vicar '. You felt on reading it that it would be a pleasant thing to be one of that Yorkshire Vicar's parishioners. You instinctively knew that he would behave towards you with kindness, tolerance and broad Christian charity; that he would take an amiable interest in all your doings, especially if you could put down an over or two from the lych-gate end; and that he would be mercifully blind to your faults, however repulsive, unless, of course, you dropped slip catches off his own bowling. One must not press Christian charity too far. . . .

Who is the Happy Cricketer, who is he? Our ' Country Vicar ' had played cricket ever since his nurse had bowled to him on the croquet lawn, and had watched the game since a rugger accident robbed him of his cricket blue at Cambridge. Every ball, every stroke, every moment of play must have given him an innocent delight which is rare in human existence. Such a man is truly a happy man. He is also a fortunate man, for he has a temperament which enables him to make each day in life a joy. Blessed are the pure in heart.

Who is the happy cricketer on the field itself? I should not say that this happy temperament is the highest quality a cricketer could have. In cricket, as in so many other fields of human endeavour, the first requisites are courage and the game's own skill. The thing that is called a Test match temperament includes both of these, plus a certain ability, which is both national and individual, to rise to the great occasion. Unconsciously the true Test player adds a cubit to his stature. Something in the man rises to the sharper challenge. This kind of player has a habit of playing for England a little better than he ever played for his county. Such men were Herbert Sutcliffe and Maurice Leyland, and, before and since, there have been many others. From Richard Barlow to Trevor Bailey they will always be there. . . .

The temperament I am thinking of, however, is not that imperturbable Test match temperament, but that admittedly less important quality which enjoys every moment of the game and conveys that enjoyment to others; a sort of infectious light-hearted gaiety which spreads from the crease to the crowd. Not every great cricketer has this: some have been dour, carrying their burdens with perhaps excessive gravity, and some have been so keenly self-critical that the least lapse from perfection has made them suffer agonies. Some take the game too seriously, forgetting that it *is* a game. The battle may rage so fiercely that enjoyment is temporarily forgotten amid the blood and sweat and toil and tears. This is a pity.

Your dour player, even on occasion your dull player, may be a valuable member of his side. It would be treason to deny this. But your happy cricketer is a joy for ever. Among the old Yorkshire cricketers stand out the names of Tom Emmett and George Ulyett. Of the two, Tom (' First a wide and then a wicket ') Emmett is the better known, but George Ulyett, commonly known as Happy Jack, is equally entitled to renown, for he was not merely happy, but the cause of happiness in others. He came from Crabtree, a pleasant village, not far from Sheffield—and he first played for a senior team by pretending to be older than he was. " I went from sixteen to eighteen in two days," he said. His gay and rollicking temperament won him golden opinions from Bramall Lane to Bendigo. Wherever he went, jokes, like Jack and Jill, went tumbling after. He said that Yorkshire played him for his good behaviour and his whistling, though (now that he came to think of it) he could also bowl and bat a bit. This was a typical bit of Ulyett under-statement, because, after playing as a colt in 1873, he lived to go in first for England with W. G. Grace and to bowl with devastating effect against the Australians. The critics of his time acclaimed him as the finest

all-round professional Yorkshire ever had and, always excepting
Hirst and Rhodes, that may well be so. When Lord (then the
Hon. M. B.) Hawke took over the Yorkshire captaincy, Ulyett
was the professional on whom he relied, just as George Hirst
became his ' senior N.C.O.' at a later date. George Hirst told
me not long ago: " He was Old George when I was Young
George. He used to call me ' young 'un '. He was a terror for
joking, but no young pro. ever had a better friend." (How
many young cricketers have I not heard say the same of George
Hirst himself?)

Ulyett enjoyed every hit he made, and he was the first
Englishman to make two fifties in a Test match. Big, handsome
and jolly, he bowled with all his heart and soul and every
ounce of his fourteen-stone body. He once said with a
grimace: " Look at poor me: if I am not slogging my hardest
I am either bowling out or throwing my right arm! " But he
only pretended to grumble. In reality he loved every minute
of it. There have been few more destructive performances
than his spell against the Australians in 1884, when he took
seven for 36. As for his fielding, the courage and zest of it
became a legend in his own lifetime. When Barlow said to
him: " Get back, Jack; I wouldn't like to kill thee," Ulyett
laughed: " If tha did, Dick, I'd be t'first tha'd killed with hard
hitting." His catch of Bonnor off his own bowling in 1886 was
a topic of pavilion conversation whenever the incredulous met
together. One sympathizes a little with the six-foot-six Bonnor,
who seems to have been fated to be dismissed by brilliantly
impossible catches. Six years before, he had been out to a
catch by Fred Grace off a ball that towered up into the sky
while the batsmen ran frantically. The distance was over a
hundred yards on the ground, but this was before the days of
anti-aircraft height-finders, and nobody ever measured how
far up it went. And nobody knows what passed through
Fred's mind during the interminable time in which the ball
was coming down and down. But Fred judged and held it.
The Graces were not a family crippled with imagination.

Ulyett's catch was different. Bonnor, who was the nearest

thing to a Jessop that Australia ever produced, and was about
twice Jessop's size, went in earlier than his usual position for the
express purpose of knocking Ulyett off his length. He hit a
swashing four and then put all his force into an even more
violent blow. As the crowd gaped round to see where it had
landed beyond them, Ulyett shot out a hand. There was a
crack like a pistol shot and the ball travelled no further. He
said himself that the ball came back at him exactly as if it had
been attached to elastic. The oldest member of the M.C.C.
sent for him, gave him a sovereign, and told him it was the
finest catch he had ever seen in the course of his long life.
This was high praise. W. G. Grace told Ulyett he was a dam'
fool ever to have attempted the catch, which might have
snapped his wrist like a stick. This was praise still higher,
coming from so eminent an anatomical authority.

Ulyett travelled wherever cricket had travelled before; he
went five times to Australia and once to South Africa and
America. At San Francisco he came across a baseball pitcher
who 'jerked' him out in the first innings, but in the second
Ulyett had the measure of him. "The pitcher nearly pitched
his arm away, while I made 160 odd not out, and I wished he'd
pitch at both ends."

From his trip to South Africa comes the classic story of Happy
Jack and the four-gallon jar. Clasping, like Mr. Pickwick, his
'lovely burden in his arms', he stumped up the ship's gangway
and was accosted by a couple of ships' officers: "What have
you got there?" "The heat out there is breaking all the bats,"
whispered Jack confidentially. "This is linseed oil to oil 'em
with." And that is how four gallons of contraband Scotch
whisky went on tour for England.

His trips to Australia and New Zealand were punctuated
with picaresque adventure. It was not so much that funny
things happened to Happy Jack as that Happy Jack happened
to things. In the harbour of a port called Bourke, while fooling
in a launch with an Australian friend, he fell backward into the
water and swam comfortably about while the launch reversed
its engine to turn and pick him up. There was a cry of:

" Look out! There's a shark! " Jack dived and swam under water for a time, watching the shark's movements. He even got out his knife to be ready for any attack, but the shark turned away and Jack was able to seize the rope thrown out to him and clamber aboard. " Afterwards," he said, " you wouldn't believe the tales people told about my Desperate Knife-Fight with the Cruel Monster of the Deep, but the truth is my only hardship was the loss of a pair of elastic-sided boots which I kicked off to swim easier. Pity I hadn't a pencil or I'd have addressed 'em back home to Sheffield."

The tour to New Zealand in 1876–77, which preceded the first of all Test matches, was a saga of misadventures. The team—there were only twelve of them—had a coach journey of 200 miles to Christchurch which included a journey in torrential rain across a flooded river-bed about 70 yards wide. This was another of the times when Jack had to swim, nor was there any comfort for the half-drowned, for the only shelter they could find for the night was an old ramshackle hut, where five lucky ones slept on the bed and the rest on the wet floor. " We drank everything there was in the place," said Jack, " bar water."

Starting off again at five the next morning, they encountered a landslide and were obliged to return to the wooden hut, which they had picked clear of food. The owner of the shanty went off and shot a sheep—whose?—and the cricketers roasted it on the smoky fire. Jack, the resourceful Yorkshireman, made oven-bottom cake (only there was no oven) with flour and water and no yeast, turning the macabre mixture elegantly over in the embers with a hay-fork.

Eventually they reached their destination, not twenty-four hours, but five minutes, before the match was due to start, and they were so tired, wet and cramped, not to say bogged down by Happy Jack's oven-bottom cake, that they could neither bowl nor field properly. The home side won the toss, batted all day, and put up a score so big that in the evening the local betting against the English team was heavy. This was unlucky for the New Zealanders, but in a sense it served them right.

After the horrors of the journey and the nightmare of the dopey day in the field, Happy Jack saw that there was only one thing for it. He agreed to be the team's spokesman in approaching their captain.

" We shall have to have a champagne supper," he said.

Lillywhite, perhaps grudgingly, agreed and, following a champagne supper and a blissful night's sleep, the English players virtually flayed the local Eighteen alive. It was not long afterwards that they crossed back over to Australia to play what is now reckoned the first of all Test matches and, owing to one thing and another, they left their wicket-keeper, Pooley, in custody. His incarceration, which was quite unjust, was not unconnected with disputes about bets on the Christchurch match, and it showed what a strain was put on a travelling side. Nowadays the M.C.C. sends out sixteen or even seventeen men. Warner's victorious team of 1903–04 numbered only fourteen. Lillywhite's men in 1876–77 were a bare dozen. There was no margin for rest, for injuries, or for such eventualities as leaving your stumper in gaol.

As well as appearing in the first Test match, Happy Jack played in what many consider the most famous one, the ill-starred ' Ashes ' game at the Oval in 1882. On England's defeat in this historic game Ulyett had his own views, which, broadly, were that the England side allowed itself to be intimidated. " After all," he said, " we only wanted 85 to win, and me and the Doctor got half of 'em." If anybody was nervous, it was not Happy Jack.

He had a poor benefit—Yorkshire finished off their opponents much too quickly—but the sums given by the grateful as personal tributes in the subscription list brought in twice as much, and in the end he received over £1,000, which in Queen Victoria's Jubilee year was real money. When he retired he settled down to keep a pub.

All his life he had been a laughing philosopher. He laughed when he made two fifties in a Test. He laughed when he made a duck. He laughed when he waded through flooded rivers in New Zealand. He laughed again when an angry mob of two thousand invaded the pitch at Sydney to deal faithfully with a Melbourne umpire and, as it appeared, to lynch the whole England eleven. Whoever were afraid that day, there were three who were not: Lord Harris, 'Monkey' Hornby and George Ulyett. The leader of the larrikins struck at Lord Harris. "Let me have a go at him," cried Ulyett, fighting his way with a stump to his captain's side.

"No, no, George," replied Lord Harris, coolly, "we are going to do nothing wrong."

'Monkey' Hornby, however, came up at the double, grabbed the larrikin, and used him as a battering ram to fight his way towards a policeman. So light-heartedly did Happy Jack take this ugly episode that immediately afterwards he perpetrated an outrageous imputation on the courage of Tom Emmett, who had gone to the pavilion to change his socks.

"Where's Tom? Oh, the crowd gave him such a fright he was seen running like a madman towards the Harbour. . . ."

Ulyett was, like Schofield Haigh at a later day, the kindest of friends and the wickedest of leg-pullers, even to the point of planting property snakes in Tom's cricket boots.

In the Sheffield pub over which Happy Jack presided there must have been much laughter and good fellowship, for no man could be miserable in that landlord's jocund company. But evil fate, which seems to detest the defiance of a happy man, struck him down, the third of the old Yorkshire cricketers to die of pneumonia. He went to a match at Bramall Lane on one of those cold and miserable days that bedevil early summer in the north. The dank chill of the day struck through his bones and, when he met George Hirst on the pavilion steps, he was unbearably depressed.

"Young 'un," he said, "I'm finished. . . ."

"Nay," cried Hirst. "Never in this world. . . ."

But it was so. A day or two later Happy Jack died suddenly and (heaven knows) prematurely at the age of forty-seven. The shades in which his gay, brave spirit wanders will be lighter than they ever were before.

2

If professional cricketers to-day are a less light-hearted race
than that which bred Tom Emmett and Happy Jack Ulyett,
who shall blame them? They live in a less light-hearted age.
They have grammar school educations inside their heads and
widely advertised unguents on top. They are seldom to be
seen like the great Lumpy Stevens dancing a jig with a mug of
ale in their hands. They have many fine qualities but, with
rare exceptions, joyousness is not in their repertoire. Right at
the top of this list of exceptions stands Yorkshire's J. H. Wardle.

I have a perhaps irrational prejudice against those writers
who appear to court the envy of the multitude by referring to
the eminent by their Christian names, if possible in diminutive
form. Pretended familiarity with the great is the most ancient
of snobberies, especially in its modern form. I may be wrong,
but I do not feel that the cause of Democracy is served by
calling archbishops Pat or Mick. To me there is something
essentially discourteous about vicarious back-slapping. But
with Wardle (J. H.) I am defeated. It would be difficult, even
on short acquaintance, to call him anything but Johnny. On
the field and off he seems to me the happiest cricketer alive.
Johnny's laughter is a tonic to fellow-players and spectators
alike.

Like the hyena in the story, Johnny would, at first sight,
appear to have very little to laugh at. He has played for
England, done well, and then been dropped in a manner which
would try the soul of any but the most even-tempered philosopher. He has, without extravagant praise or, at any rate,
with much less praise than he deserves, borne for a long time the
major burden of his county's bowling. He is not Wilfred
Rhodes. He is not Hedley Verity. But he keeps on, gets
through an inordinate amount of work in a season, and takes
his 150 wickets with almost monotonous regularity. Nobody
says what a splendid slow bowler he is, or that his action is like
Frank Woolley's. Nobody even reproves his gluttony for work.
It's only Johnny.

B 2

He is that rare thing in any walk of life, a genuine humorist, and, like a true humorist's, his tales are mostly against himself. In his early days his batting stance came in for criticism, and great pains were taken at Headingley to improve the position of his feet. Somebody asked him afterwards: " Did they get your feet right? "

" They did an' all," said Johnny; " so right they walked me straight into t'second team."

After a gruelling day of almost fruitless toil at Scarborough in which he had bowled himself virtually to a standstill, he was having a drink with Maurice Leyland.

" You know," he said ruefully, " every time I bowl a bad ball I could kick myself."

" Could you now? " said Maurice sympathetically. " Nay, Johnny, tha must be black and blue."

But when he tells that tale himself he shouts with laughter!

His capacity for laughter helps him to go on bowling when most of the others would have been tired out. At Worcester in 1953 he sent down 76 overs, i.e. 456 balls, including 29 maidens, and took 5 wickets for 136 runs. This is not quite a record for the West Indian, A. L. Valentine, bowled 92 overs in England's second innings at Nottingham in 1950, but it at any rate gives a picture of a man who will never give in. He is just as unwilling to capitulate when he is batting. His more facetious friends— he has no enemies—say that he has only two strokes: one is hitting a six and the other is getting out trying to hit another six. But this, like most wisecracks, is an over-simplification. And he has hit a lot of sixes. His conviction when he goes in at, say, No. 9, is that his side's innings is by no means over.

" They'll have to fight for it," says Johnny, and on this assumption, Yorkshire often (and England sometimes) have put up a much more impressive total than they might reasonably have expected. He has proved, as did Happy Jack, that the stubborn fighting quality of Yorkshire can go just as well with a smile as with a scowl.

When nothing serious is at stake, Wardle will entertain the crowd with a little clowning, which as described, does not seem funny, but as seen, brings roars of laughter. During one of the games of the 1953 Scarborough Festival, Hutton had reason to change his bat while at the crease. Wardle ran out from the pavilion with two for Hutton to choose from. In the usual way, Len tried one and Johnny tried one. Johnny apparently leant on his too hard. It broke clean in two, leaving him with the splice and handle in his hand. The crowd rocked at his exaggerated astonishment. It was obviously a put-up job.

Before the start of the 1953 season proper, a floodlit cricket match was played for charity on Bradford Northern's Rugby League ground. The pitch was in the centre and the goal-posts were still standing. While fielding, Johnny chased a ball which went perilously near goal, went on running when he had picked it up and scored a beautiful solo try between the posts. It was the comedian's quick-change. But I have never known Johnny clown, when clowning was wrong.

Johnny has a charming wife and two small sons of almost terrifying vitality, who eagerly compete for the honour of chastisement when one of their more outrageous exploits comes to light. I do not know how far their technical skill has advanced, but between them, they have a Test match temperament already.

In their Middlesex match at Lord's in 1952 Yorkshire won the toss and started well. Hutton carved for himself a lapidary century and Lowson's fifty was, on the leg side at any rate, almost as good as his master's. After the openers went, there was a horrid little collapse, and the score went from 220 for one to about 240 for five It was left to that honest journeyman Harry Halliday to pull the game round. He achieved his task with courage, obstinacy and patience, but this patience found no echo in the responses of the Lord's congregation, and by the time Mr. Halliday's entirely worthy and worthwhile effort had ended, the whole ground—I do not defend its attitude—had sunk into a slough of bored exasperation. At 6.26 Wardle (J. H.) came out of the pavilion, striding down the steps with the air of a man who says to himself: " Only a couple of overs to go: what a pity I can't get more than 72 off 'em."

CHAPTER III

OLD MASTERS, NEW BOYS

I

ONE argument that never ends is the quarrel between the old and the new—any old old and any old new. Almost everybody you know will cheerfully line up on one side or the other and hit out. A social survey would almost certainly elicit the conviction (held by everybody else) that everybody (*a*) under or (*b*) over forty should be shot. Yet this controversy, so pleasing to nearly everybody, is invariably beside the point. One of the few certain things I think I have learnt in a largely ignorant life is this: that nothing is either good or bad because it is old or new. If it is true that the old have once been young, it is equally true that the young will in time be old. This alone should convince us that the old and new are very much alike; indeed, they are only the same people or things at different times.

When we compare old and new generals, old and new writers, or old and new cricketers, we must make an attempt to be fair. We must take account of the different conditions under which each does his stuff and, above all, we must remember that we are comparing someone who has reached the shining peak of achievement with someone who is still moving up from the base camp. Therefore it is fair to say: " Tom Graveney is a potential Hammond." Some critics would prefer to say with wholly unjustifiable dogmatism: " Graveney will never be another Hammond. . . ." They would be wrong. At the very best, nobody knows. It is legitimate to hope and it is certain that the young will come along. They always have.

C. B. FRY

In his brilliant short biography, Denzil Batchelor calls C. B. Fry the *magnifico*. The title suggests a colourful picture,

45

but it is, if anything, an understatement. In his many-sided magnificence, Fry is the answer to that minor but distressing symptom of this age, the petty specialist, the man who " doesn't know anything else," for Fry is not merely a supremely talented individual; he is a one-man Ministry of All the Talents. Cricket, what is cricket? In the words of his friend, the charming writer, Clifford Bax, it is a beautiful but difficult game. But outstanding ability to play it is only one of Fry's accomplishments, and he has been far more than a master-batsman in a master-age. He has always done a dozen things better than most people to-day do one thing. What manner of man is this Fry? A Senior scholar of Wadham College, his Oxford record reads: First Class Moderations, Honours in Literae Humaniores. Here is a genuine classical scholar, an all-round athlete whose long-jump world-record lasted nearly half a century, a man devoted above all to the high task of training young sailor-citizens, author of one of the finest and most finely-titled autobiographies of our time, Prince Ranjitsinhji's friend and colleague at the League of Nations, and almost a King of Albania.

What a Ruritanian romance went west when Fry glanced that offer to leg! If he had accepted the crown I will wager he would have turned that wild and wilful kingdom into a well-ordered and prosperous little country on the lines of Holland or Denmark. It would have had an efficient Navy and it would have sent a Test team regularly to England. . . . Whenever I read about Marshal Tito, so handsome, so forceful, so knowledgeable of his own mind and so defiant of the big battalions, I toy with the fancy that, but for the difference in generations, someone of the calibre of C. B. Fry must have gone to Eastern Europe after all and is, by sheer strength of character, making certain that at least one country is better governed than the rest of those rather grim parts.

My present rather slavish admiration is a thing that has grown through the years from an unpromising start. Fifty years ago I hated the man. As a boy I have sat, clasping my grubby knees, and praying that fire from heaven might fall upon the maker of so many centuries against Yorkshire. When, in the long field, he would run fifty yards, pick up a flying ball and throw down the wicket in a single superb action, I did not recognize that here was a subject for Phidias. I merely turned to my neighbour and scornfully muttered: " Swank! " This, I am now willing to concede, was a non-objective attitude.

For a long period of years he was known to all Englishmen as C. B. Ranji called him Charlo. Only the great W. G. called him Charlie. As a batsman, he was not as graceful as Palairet or Spooner, but in the hard facts of life dominance takes precedence over grace. The question is, as Humpty-Dumpty said, who shall be master. He *mastered* bowlers and lorded it over them on every kind of wicket. His concentration on each ball of the day was unrelenting. If he made a stroke that did not please him, he would make it again, this time correctly, while the fielders waited. He once said that the critics complained he had only two strokes. " They were wrong," said Fry; " I only had one, but it went in twenty-two directions."

His records are gargantuan and the figures for his batting career between 1892 and 1921 are as impressive as any long-term figures I know:

Innings	Aggregate	Not out	Highest score	Centuries	Average
658	30,886	43	258	94	50·22

How many batsmen of that classic period have an average of over 50? Many of the greatest names have one of considerably less. In 1947, a glorious summer, Denis Compton made eighteen centuries but, I would say, without disrespect to one of my contemporary favourites, that when Fry made thirteen centuries, six of them in succession, in 1901, the bowling was better. The attack was an intensive bombardment. You will find the names of Hirst, Rhodes, Haigh, Lockwood, Richardson, Walter Mead, Blythe, Kortright, J. T. Hearne, Arnold, Fielder, Braund and S. M. J. Woods among the opposition, and I think this proves that Fry's task was the harder. Ten years afterwards he made four centuries in succession. Four times in his career he made a century in each innings, and three times he missed this feat by one run. If my young heart had been laid bare in 1904, the figures 177 and 229 might have been found written on it. Those were the scores C. B. Fry made against Yorkshire in that year. The intellectual concentration which made all these vast scores possible was all the more remarkable in that it was exercised by a man who had many interests in life and who, so far from being a dour, brow-knitting type, was of a mercurial and ebullient temperament.

Not merely did he live through the golden age of cricket; he was up at Oxford during a classic period. I smile sadly when I read every now and then of some unfortunate under-graduate who has rowed a little or played a little football and in consequence has had to be sent down because he has not found time for any work. Fry was the best man of his period at cricket, athletics, and both codes of football. And he took a first in pure Classics. Of his Oxford friends he has said : " F. E. Smith was the wittiest; John Simon was the most lucid; but Belloc was my hero." It was of Belloc, too, that he said : " Perfect prose is rarely written by anyone who cannot think in French." The brilliant F. E. once said when visiting the *Mercury*: " This is a fine show, C. B., but, for you, a back-water." " Yes," Fry replied, " but the question remains whether it is better to be successful . . . or happy." C. B. Fry has been happy *and* successful.

Of C. B. Fry's life-long friendship with Prince Ranjitsinhji this is not the place to write. Seldom on the cricket field, or anywhere else, can there have been a partnership so prolific in runs—or ideas. Even the League of Nations seemed on a sound basis when those two were at Geneva. If the world had not been an incorrigibly stupid place well past praying for, those two together would almost have put it right in their time. And Fry has always maintained that if the Government of the day had listened to Ranji and himself, the British might well still be in India.

For some reason, perhaps partly because he was an excellent fast bowler, critics spread the legend that, before meeting

Ranji, his batting talent was meagre. The notion that he was a bat who bettered himself merely by watching Ranji is, of course, nonsense. When he said: " I was a bad bat; I had merely made a lot of runs," the tone of his voice should have been noted. Ranji, as a cricketer, was unique; his lightning glance, his sinuous grace will never come to us again. But Fry, as the scholar athlete was, and is, unique, too. Nobody, certainly no classical scholar, has ever played so many games so well.

And no living person has ever given more single-hearted devotion to an idea than did Fry, in his forty-two years of running the training ship *Mercury*, to the task of turning picked working-class lads into possible Naval officers. His heart was never far from those sailor lads. Asked if, given the chance, he would have lived his life differently, he once replied: " Yes, I would like to have joined the Navy and become an Admiral." He said, too, that he was prouder of having had two poems in the middle page of *The Times* than of anything else he had done. On that occasion he had also something profound to say on the subject of leadership. " In England," he said, " you absorb and represent the ideas of the people, if you wish to lead them. . . ."

Not being of the company of the meek, he has not yet inherited the earth. His mind is forthright, his comment is pungent. He has a reputation of not suffering fools gladly. Yet the foreword to this book proves that he has suffered at least one, and for his personal kindness to me I can never be sufficiently grateful. Once, in rather deprecating the fuss made about cricket, he wrote: " A beautiful game, but not as good as polo. . . ."

I do not know whether C. B. Fry ever really did play polo. If he did, I will swear he mastered it as eagerly and surely as the Maltese Cat.

J. T. TYLDESLEY

Cricket has inspired much pleasant verse and at least one great poem. In that poignantly nostalgic lyric my nobler namesake cried out: " *O my Hornby and my Barlow long ago* . . . ' Hornby and Barlow were the great Lancashire opening batsmen of the 'seventies and 'eighties, but they were not the heroes of Lancashire's greatest period. If we reckon Lancashire's (and almost every other county's) greatest period as being the turn of the century, then Lancashire's finest opening batsmen consisted of, not Hornby and Barlow, but MacLaren and Spooner. Furthermore, I doubt if any county at any time had more brilliant Nos. 1, 2 and 3 than:

> A. C. MacLaren
> R. H. Spooner
> Tyldesley (J. T.)

You may enter the competition with Yorkshire's Tunnicliffe, Brown and Denton or Surrey's Hayward, Hobbs and Hayes. Sussex cannot secure a valid entry with three; its triangle must become a quadrilateral: C. B. Fry, Vine, Killick and K. S. Ranjitsinhji. Whatever three you bring along, the Lancashire triumvirate, I think, remains supreme: MacLaren, the classic master of the upright stance, with a backlift that only Ajax could have bettered; Spooner, the elegant artist who made an innings as graceful as a minuet; and Tyldesley, J. T.—Johnnie Tyldesley. As boys we pronounced it Tiddlesley, but he went on making big scores against ' us ', whatever we called him.

The crowning glory of J. T. Tyldesley was not his aggregate of nearly 38,000 runs, his 86 centuries, or his tale of nineteen years in which he never missed making his thousand. It was the fact that in the golden age of English batting, when the roll of amateur talent (much of it genius) sounded like the muster of knights at Agincourt—L. C. H. Palairet, R. H. Spooner, A. C. MacLaren, R. E. Foster, F. S. Jackson, P. A. Perrin, and C. B. Fry—in this aristocratic company, I say, Tyldesley, J. T., held his own, and held it in the key position of No. 3. What supreme qualities had this modest north-country professional got that kept him an honoured member of this noble company? To the privilege of batting for England in those golden days few were called and fewer still were chosen. The only professional members of that virtually exclusive club were Tyldesley and Tom Hayward, and of the two only Tyldesley was there by unchallengeable right.

What took him there? First, he had a lion's heart beneath a deceptively modest and quiet exterior; then, despite the fact that he was under rather than over medium size, he had a splendid technical equipment; and, best reason of all, he was an attacker, first, last and all the time. He was not a fantastic hitter, like Jessop, but he was a true attacker. Floating somewhere in the public's subconscious mind, there is a libellous image of the symbolic professional, anxiously stooging away at the crease, stopping the straight ones, padding up to the awkward ones, and waiting for a loose one to push away to leg for a single. In every possible way, Tyldesley was different. He never stooged in his life. If he had been a Scotsman, he would have batted with a claymore. Bowling was meant to be hit, each ball of the over was sent down to be scored off. Few batsmen in any age can have had such agile footwork. We speak of a keen player as being ' on his toes '. Tyldesley literally rose on his toes to the stroke. His cutting was, after Ranji's and Trumper's, the most dazzling ever seen and often so late as to be positively posthumous. His off-drive was like a flash of light. Nor were these his only weapons against the enemy. His offside play was orthodox, if brilliant; his legside strokes were almost a form of eternal punishment. His pulling was violent and remorseless; his hooking had behind it all the strength of two splendid shoulders. He pulled as Hirst pulled, and hooked as Hendren hooked at a later date. He did not play himself in; he set about the bowling from the word GO. This owed nothing to recklessness or the accident of a quick eye. It was an attacking policy. Talking after his retirement with someone who was discussing the necessity of waiting for long hops, Tyldesley said: " Nobody ever bowled us long hops. We had to make our own." (On this same subject Fry once said: " I hardly ever remember a bad ball in a big match.") To see Tyldesley set about the bowling was to see him in the guise of a buck, a Corinthian, a lad of mettle, a swordsman of the calibre of Alan Breck. Yet the paradox of all this was that off the field he was the gentlest and kindest of men; a person of high principle, and a student who generally read a book on long train journeys while the other chaps were playing cards.

Twenty years after Tyldesley was dead I remember somebody telling a story about him. I do not remember the point of it, but it involved in the course of conversation a certain amount of damning and blasting, along with one or two cultural words now associated with the Third Programme. George Hirst, who was present, shook his head. He was not so much re- butting a slander as correcting a grave error of fact.

"Not Johnnie," he said. "He couldn't have talked like that. You never met a quieter-spoken chap in all your life."

This was characteristic of Hirst; but the picture of essential decency that it evoked must also have been highly charac- teristic of Tyldesley. Yet the most characteristic picture of all is of his batting on a bad wicket. There never was a better player in evil conditions, and only Hobbs and Trumper were anything like so good. In his career he scored 86 centuries, but none of these was so superlatively excellent as the 62 he made out of 103 in the second Test at Melbourne in 1904. This was the match in which Rhodes took fifteen wickets and Trumper made 74 and 35 out of two Australian scores of little more than a hundred. All who saw it say that Tyldesley's 62, when the wicket was at its very worst, must have been the best innings ever played by mortal man. Trumper's two knocks must have been very nearly as good.

Tyldesley had a brother sixteen years younger than himself, also a shining credit to his county, who scored his thousand runs nineteen times, made 102 centuries and piled up nearly 39,000 runs altogether. And the difference between Ernest and Johnnie was the difference between the very, very good and the great.

MacLaren said that J. T. Tyldesley was as good a bat as Trumper. Fry said that Tyldesley was nearer to Hobbs in merit than was usually supposed. Two such judges are not likely to be far wrong.

Colin Blythe

Among the famous cricketers who lost their lives in the
First World War were Major Booth, the Yorkshire all-rounder
from Pudsey, and Colin Blythe, the Kent slow bowler, who was
loved wherever he played. Nobody will ever shift me from the
opinion that Wilfred Rhodes is the best slow bowler who ever
lived, but he was not the best merely because there was in-
sufficient competition in his day. Perhaps it is absurd to speak
of the ' day ' of a cricketer who played cricket of the highest
class for over thirty years. Rhodes had at least three ' days '.
First, when he was England's best bowler; second, when he
was England's second-best bat, and, third, after the first war,
when he came back as England's best bowler once more. I am
however, talking of his first day, of the period which far more
discerning spectators than myself have agreed to call the
Golden Age.

Every county then had, as a matter of course, one tip-top
slow bowler, who was as necessary a part of the club's equipment as the horse that pulled the heavy roller. Nowadays if a
county has a good one, he is likely to be so overworked that
he may well come in time to feel that he *is* the horse that pulls
the heavy roller. If Wardle has had this feeling in the last
season or two, I could not find it in my heart to blame him,
particularly as I know for certain that he would undoubtedly
keep his tail up. But in the Golden Age there were slow
bowlers in plenty: George Cox of Sussex, father of the present
George Cox, that dashing bat and even more dashing cover-
point; George Dennett, who took 150 wickets a year a dozen
times in succession; S. G. Smith, the West Indian who played
for Northants, and Sam Hargreave of Warwickshire. And
there were several more, rich in variety and deep in cunning.

As surely as Rhodes was the greatest of them all, so surely was
Colin (or ' Charlie ') Blythe the second greatest. He was, to
begin with, a member of a popular team. After their own
county, all the boys of my time had a second favourite. Often
it was Gloucestershire, mainly because of Jessop. At any rate,

from Grace to Graveney, Gloucester have always had somebody.   Kent, too, was a pleasant, likeable county, incapable,
even before the advent of the great Frank Woolley, of serving
up dull cricket.   Its reputation was that of a team that played
with dash and impetuosity and always tried to finish its matches.
One of its chief ' finishers ' was Blythe, an eager polisher-off of
batting sides.   The best judges called him a supreme artist with
the ball.   He had a thoughtful, whimsical face, and those long,
sensitive fingers which are so often associated with the artist in
fiction but less often with the artist in real life.   He was a skilled
player on the violin, though I should not like to assert he was as
accomplished a practical performer as old Small of Hambledon,
who, meeting a vicious bull on his way to a musical party,
began ' playing upon his bass, to the admiration and perfect
satisfaction of the mischievous beast '.   At any rate, Blythe
played upon the hesitations and weaknesses of opposing batsmen with the almost diabolical skill of a Paganini.   His
bowling was one long temptation, a continuous invitation to
walk into the parlour.   He was a spider to whom it was a
positive honour to be a fly.   In certain years he was helped by
bad weather and bad wickets, but his skill in exploiting these
conditions had a touch of the uncanny.

Mr. H. S. Altham in his history of the game has said of him :

> " The very look on his face, the long, sensitive fingers, the elastic
> back sweep of the left arm before delivery, with the right hand thrown
> up in perfect balance against it, the short, dancing approach, the long
> last stride, and the final flick of the arm as it came over, all these
> spoke of a highly sensitive and nervous instrument, beautifully co-
> ordinated, directed by a subtle mind, and inspired by a natural love
> for its art. . . ."

His methods were not unlike those of Hedley Verity, who
entered into a continuous conspiracy with Arthur Mitchell to
defraud the batsman of his wicket.   There was something of the
confidence trick about the thing.   Blythe, too, had his close-to-
the-wicket confederates and, however cautious the batsman
might be, it was almost humanly impossible to prevent the ball
from popping off the edge of the bat into welcoming hands.

If you wish to look up Blythe's most spectacular performances,

you will find that he once took 17 Northamptonshire wickets
for 48 runs, and he did not take more than a day to do the job.
But it might be argued that in this instance the opposition was
not strong. His finest hour, or at any rate period, was in the
second Test of 1907 against the South African touring team.
This was a very fine side, containing nearly all the googly
bowlers in the world, and was, in a way, unlucky to lose the
series. Many unexpected, and even sinister things have happened in Tests at Leeds, usually to England, and in 1907 the
whole English team was dismissed for 76, mainly owing to the
superb slow bowling of Aubrey Faulkner, who that day was
virtually unplayable. But England had two supreme fighters:
one was the captain, C. B. Fry, who made one of the greatest
half-centuries of his career; the other was Blythe, who merci-
lessly exploited the evils of the pitch, taking eight for 59 and
seven for 40. Nobody ever knew what that effort cost him in
nervous energy. The strain upon his delicately strung frame
was terrific, for he bowled with a fanatical concentration that
brought him to the edge of a nervous breakdown. England
won by only 53 runs. A loose over or two might have turned
the scale the wrong way, but in two innings Blythe never
bowled a single bad ball.

In all the Tests in which he played he took 100 wickets for
1,863, and there was not one of those 100 wickets which did not
represent the work of a genuine artist in bowling. When he
gave his life for his country in 1917 he was thirty-eight years
old. Had he survived he might have come back and performed
more devastating bowling feats for Kent and England, for
slow bowlers do not grow old. Every year at the Canterbury
Festival, which he graced for so many seasons, himself an
essential part of its colour and gaiety, visiting teams place a
wreath on his memorial. That is a place where Colin Blythe
will ever be remembered.

Ranji, who feared few bowlers in his day, said that on the
very worst of wickets Blythe was even more difficult to play than
Rhodes. It is impossible to conceive higher praise than that.

C. J. KORTRIGHT

Colin Blythe, alas, died young, but Charles Jesse Kortright lived to a lively old age, and was eighty-one when he died at the end of 1952, the last survivor of the great fast bowlers of the Golden Age, and very possibly the fastest bowler who ever lived. But the most remarkable fact about him was not that he once bowled a ball so fast that it leaped first bounce straight out of the ground for six byes.[1] The most remarkable fact about this remarkable bowler was that he never played for England. To-day selectors would go on their knees to such a bowler. Why was he not picked then? The reason was that in the Golden Age there were excellent fast bowlers in every county and superlative ones in three or four. Surrey had Lockwood and Richardson and later Neville Knox, and Lancashire had Mold, a great smasher of stumps, and Walter Brearley, an equally great smasher of batsmen's reputations. Worcestershire had W. B. Burns, who, for a few overs, could strike terror to the boldest heart, while Derbyshire based a strong attack on Warren and Bestwick, the former of whom took 5 for 44 against the Australians in the third match of F. S. Jackson's victorious 1905 eleven. Kent had that ripe character Arthur Fielder, who, when asked if it was true that he took all ten wickets in the 1906 Gentlemen v. Players match, replied: " That's right, and eight of 'em was out."

So Kortright never got an England cap, but some of his county performances were prodigious. In 1900 he took eight for 57 against that Yorkshire side which lost only two matches in three years, and he almost always took heavy toll off Surrey batsmen, not seldom at the Oval.

Physically, he was a magnificent specimen and, when well over seventy, was tall and straight and still slim. In his heyday every ounce of his splendid strength went into the catapult of his delivery. He batted, too, with commendable violence and occasionally hit a Jessop-like century only too rare for an Essex bat. In later years he remained an eager follower of the

---

[1] The experts say this cannot be done, but Kortright said he did it.

game and a faithful supporter of his own county. He played a lot of golf and played it well, but he never let it interfere with his support for Essex cricket.

His comments on contemporary bowling techniques may have seemed unsophisticated to young county players, but they were forthrightly expressed and sincerely meant. Briefly (and pungently), he called for a return to first principles and seemed puzzled by the fact that his juniors did not bowl—at the stumps—fast, straight, good-length balls, including frequent yorkers for the innocent newcomer, all the time. He claimed that they had been led away by false doctrines and by the self-pitying feeling that bowlers nowadays were hard done by.

" You've got three stumps to go at," said Kortright. " What more do you want? "

One of the classic apocryphal stories of W. G. Grace concerns three balls sent down to that reluctant crease-leaver by C. J. Kortright. Kortright bowled his usual lightning ball. It struck W. G. on the pad. The bowler appealed, the Doctor frowned, the umpire shook his head. Kortright sent down a second ball, equally fast. There was an audible click. The wicket-keeper appealed, the Doctor glared, the umpire shook his head. Kortright thundered up on his long run and hurled down the ball of a lifetime. It knocked the middle stump out of the ground and sent the leg stump drunkenly staggering. The Doctor glowered, the umpire shrugged. Then the Doctor began slowly to walk away.

" Surely you're not going, Doctor," said Kortright with a sunny smile; " there's one stump still standing."

I should like that to have been a Tom Emmett story, but great is truth and it shall prevail.

Kortright is reputed to have said, even boasted, that he never did a day's work in his life. But if being the fastest bowler in history is not hard work I do not know what is.

2

Compared with the old masters, my new boys look extremely new. Most Englishmen are modest in their opinions. They do not claim to know better than everybody, only better than the English selectors. Their opinions are blunt and forthright. My opinions, on the other hand, are positively pusillanimous, for of the four new boys I have chosen here, the 1953 selectors had as high an opinion as my own. Foolish critics find Test players on every bush. Clever critics like to hedge their bets, and wise critics are cautiously hopeful. The following, as they say, are well spoken of: M. C. Cowdrey of Oxford and Kent, whom I saw play for Tonbridge at Lord's when he looked extraordinarily young; Robin Marlar, Cambridge's 1953 captain, a tricky off-break bowler and an obviously ebullient personality; Ken Suttle of Sussex, a genuinely promising left-hander with some Harvey-like qualities; and P. J. Loader, a tall young fastish bowler who on several occasions has done good things for Surrey while Alec Bedser has been doing good work for England. And there are three Middlesex lads—the fast bowler, Alan Moss, and the two young all-rounders, Fred Titmus and Don Bennett—of whom at least one former England captain thinks a great deal. And here I should like to set it on record that, among the young cricketers that I have met of recent years, I have found exactly those qualities which elderly gentlemen so often fail to find in the present generation. I have found them, almost without exception, modest, well-mannered, conscientious and as keen as any previous generation ever was. In any event, whatever hopes and fears there have been about many of the young entry, there can be few doubts about the young man who has successfully staked his claim to go in at No. 3 for Surrey and England.

P. B. H. May

Tall, good-looking, confident and accomplished, Peter May was regularly hitting centuries at school; one in 1946 and three in 1947, when he captained the eleven and had an average of over 80. He was born on the last day of 1929 and started cricket early. From Charterhouse he did not go up to Cambridge. Instead, he went straight into the Royal Navy to do his National Service. Now, there has to be something special about a young man who not merely wishes, but is thought good enough, to do his National Service in the Navy, for it is the most choosy of the three Services. It does not particularly like conscription and, while it has the pick of everybody, it will not settle for just anybody. May must have done well in his training to be allowed to play cricket regularly, and he showed his gratitude to the naval authorities by hitting up several fine scores, including a century and a not-out half century against the Royal Air Force at Lord's and a century in each innings for Combined Services against Worcestershire.

When he eventually went up to Cambridge, his batting was seen to be of distinguished quality even among such prolific scorers as Sheppard and Hubert Doggart. Even when May did not make big scores—and he made plenty—he had the stamp of the real cricketer upon him. He seemed, when I first saw him, to have all the strokes that I had been taught long ago to admire and, as if to please my prejudices, to be exceptionally eager in attempting all those handsome ones on the off side. I have seen some comparatively small scores from Peter May, but never a bad innings.

In 1951 he played in two Tests against the South African team, joining the happy few who have scored a century on their first appearance for their country. In that year he began to develop the cheerful habit of making two hundreds in a match, with 167 and 103 not out for Surrey against Essex at Southend and 174 and 100 not out for the M.C.C. against Yorkshire. There was more in this than merely the seaside air.

In 1952 he reached an even higher level, not necessarily of quality, but of practical success, making ten centuries, a total surpassed only by Hutton, who made eleven. In the first-class batting averages for this season he was second with 62, a little below his friend David Sheppard, who was top with 64, and a little above Hutton, the best batsman in the world, who was third with 61. May's fielding, either in the slips, at cover, or in the deep, was unexceptionable.

Early in 1953 he fell, as the best players in the history of the game have occasionally done, into an unlucky patch. Such patches, like death and Schedule D, are the common lot. He played in the first Test against the Australians at Nottingham and was unfortunate to be out, snapped at the wicket, for a small score in semi-darkness. The selectors in their wisdom—and I believe it *was* wisdom—left him out until the fifth Test at the Oval, and there, on his own ground, he played two grand innings, not of size but of value at critical moments, justifying his reinstatement beyond reasonable argument.

A spectator does not go to a cricket match as a punter goes to the races. There may be more excitement, if you like that sort of thing, in three minutes' racing than in three days' cricket. It all depends on the kind of excitement you want. You may win, or much more probably lose, money at racing. You will not win money at cricket, except in the sense that to enjoy a day's sunshine, fresh air, good company, art, drama and, iust possibly, heart disease for two bob is surely a financial bargain. If it is, hurra for the profit motive! But at both games you can pick winners. Not all fulfil their early promise. Not many cricketers, as May did, make a century in their first Test. Only one horse wins the Derby in any given year and no horse wins it twice. It may be just as difficult to pick a winner in Test cricket as in the Grand National (the one racing man of my acquaintance once solemnly told me that this was ' nothing but a gamble '). But if you pick a true cricket winner you can sit back and draw dividends of pleasure for the next twenty years. And Peter May is my idea of such a winner.

T. W. GRAVENEY

I am not quite so sure about Tom Graveney as I am about Peter May, but I am pretty sure. The astonishing, and most attractive, thing about Gloucestershire is not its glittering succession of great names, but the fact that each of those names should in turn find a successor at all. Grace, Jessop, Hammond, and then what? Again, the wonder is not that Graveney does not yet wear the mantle of Hammond with tailor-made ease, but that it should have fallen on a young man without knocking him flat.

The West Country has always had a reputation for spacious and animated cricket. Jessop was unique in any county, but to go no farther back, men like Barnett, Gimblett and Tremlett —diminutive by name but not by nature—are typical of the spirit of bright aggression in which cricket is played in the West. The present idol of every Gloucestershire schoolboy from eight to eighty is Tom Graveney. If you were to see him piling up runs at Bristol at a great pace with apparently effortless ease, you would say: " Ah, here is the typical West Country lad." And you would be wrong, for Tom was born just twenty-seven years ago in Northumberland, a county renowned for many virtues but not particularly for cricket. His people soon came south, however, first to Lancashire and then to Bristol, where he and his older brother Kenneth went to the Grammar School. Here Tom, the England batsman, was a bowler and Ken, that excellent bowler who took ten wickets in an innings against Derbyshire in 1949, was a batsman.

Some boys are natural ball-game players—it seems most unfair to the others—and there was hardly any game within his reach at which Tom Graveney was not adept: he must have been a hard and heavy fellow to tackle at Rugger and, what seems more extraordinary, he was good enough at golf to have taken a professional job.

The war played havoc with the careers of young cricketers, as with those of others, but perhaps Graveney did not suffer as badly as most. He volunteered for the Army before his actual call-up and spent the latter part of the war in the Middle East, where, on one kind of pitch or another, a good deal of cricket was to be enjoyed.

When young Captain Graveney came back from the war he found himself, surely a rare prospect for soldiers from the wars returning, a prospective candidate for three professional careers: cricket, golf and accountancy. He considered them in that order and plumped for cricket. From 1948, when he began with Gloucestershire, his career has been one of steady progress, if not triumph. He first played for England in 1951, and up to the end of the 1953 season had made fourteen Test appearances

altogether. Some would say that his best innings was in the
Lord's Test in 1953, when he helped his captain to put on 168
in a style worthy of the master against an Australian attack
that was made to look far less than mighty. Others, and they
are not necessarily wrong, speak of his innings played against
the South Africans in 1951 on a nasty wicket at—where do you
think?—Manchester. I forget his score. I think it was
15. . . .

There are some people who have mistrusted what they called
his ' moods '; that is to say, his cricketing moods, which is
perhaps only a way of saying that there are times when his
concentration appears to falter. Of this surely the worst that
can be said is that it has occasionally happened to players of
much greater experience. Some, too, have said that earlier
on there was a certain lackadaisical quality in his fielding, but
those who saw him in the Australians' second innings at
Nottingham dismiss Alan Davidson with one of the finest
running catches ever seen on that ground could never agree.
As for being lackadaisical, before going off to the West Indies
on last winter's tour he was training as hard as could be every
day with Bristol Rovers. There are few players to-day who
give as much pleasure to themselves and to enlightened spectators as does Tom Graveney, with his formidable back-lift
and his lovely off-drive, on top of his form. Go, mark him
well. Let no such man be distrusted.

G. A. R. LOCK

How many Test-winning left-arm slow bowlers has England
had in the last half century? Remarkably few. Two were
from Yorkshire: Rhodes, the greatest, who took 127 wickets in
all Tests, and the lamented Hedley Verity, who took the greatest
number, 144; and two were from Kent: Colin Blythe, who
took exactly 100, and the incomparable Frank Woolley, who,
though he became even more renowned as one of the most
beautiful left-handed batsmen of all time, took as many as 89.
It used to be said that every perambulator between Laisterdyke
and Liversedge contained a potential England slow left-arm

bowler. Alas, it must be the quality of post-war prams. . . .
No heaven-born slow bowler has burst upon the West Riding,
except perhaps Johnny Wardle, who would not claim to be
heaven-sent. He merely took four wickets for 7 in the Manchester Test in 1953 and, so far as one can judge, scared the
selectors into dropping him.

The outstanding slow bowler of 1952 and 1953 was undoubtedly G. A. R. (Tony) Lock, the young Surrey left-
hander, who was born at Limpsfield twenty-five years ago.
In the last two years of Surrey's triumph in the county championship three factors were evident: inspired and forceful
captaincy, brilliant near-wicket fielding, and the spectacle of
three bowlers near the top of the table. For the first, high
praise is due to Stuart Surridge, the most vital and dynamic
county captain since Brian Sellars; to the second and third
Lock made a solid contribution, both as a candidate for *felo de se*
at short fine leg and as one, with Alec Bedser and Laker, of
Surrey's triumvirate of regular hundred-wicket takers. This
question of bat-end fielding is immensely important. Failure
in this semi-suicidal art can lose Test matches; success can win
them. If, during those two years, Lock had not been the best
available slow bowler in the country he might well have been
worth his place in an England eleven for his valour at suicide
corner. In 1952 he shared, with his equally dauntless county
captain, 112 (one hundred and twelve) catches at the cannon's
mouth. I cannot be certain, without the relevant reference
material, but I should doubt very much whether any two
fieldsmen, neither being a wicket-keeper, have ever brought
down such a bag. In 1953 Lock's catching was equally
courageous, but selectors and captains have to face this position:
that if you persistently put one of your best bowlers in a place
which is practically the equivalent of being shot against a wall,
sooner or later he will damage a finger, if no worse. This is
what actually happened in 1953. A damaged finger kept him
out of the first three Tests and threw doubt upon his appearance
in the fifth up to the last moment. But the result atoned for the
anxiety. All the world knows how vital a contribution his five

wickets for 45 in the Australian second innings made to victory in game and rubber.

Accuracy, which was in the very blood of the old ones, has not been an outstanding characteristic of post-war slow left-handers. Lock's accuracy has been teasing and persistent. This is the quality and prerogative of the veteran and, when a young man achieves it early in his career, he is likely to grow better and better in other matters, too. There was a flurry of unpleasant excitement in 1952 when, in Surrey's second match against the touring Indians, Lock was no-balled by Price, the square-leg umpire, for alleged throwing. It was a courageous action on the part of the umpire, who naturally stuck to his decision when hooted by a section of the gasometer crowd. It is always a difficult or an embarrassing business to no-ball a well-known bowler. Sometimes it is done as a test case is brought in the law courts. There were some ' slinging ' bowlers whom batsmen gunned for over long periods, as Lord Harris did for Crossland of Lancashire. One famous and powerful umpire, one Phillips, once had the temerity to no-ball the great Ernest (' Sorry, Doc, she slipped! ') Jones. This episode had about it an almost staggering quality, and its effect was profounder than anybody could have imagined. One of the most sacred of Australia's cricket legends concerns a Sunday school teacher who asked her pupils: " What was the most surprising episode in the life of Jonah? " And the answer was: " When he was no-balled by Jim Phillips."

Great bowlers have been no-balled in their time; some have had to give up the game, some have mended their ways and lived to bowl again. . . . In spite of his occasional aberration here and in the West Indies, I am convinced that there is nothing in Lock's action that cannot be permanently cured.

F. S. TRUEMAN

When visitors to Yorkshire venture the opinion that young Fred Trueman is a second Harold Larwood, the natives sup up their beer and gaze into the middle distance. They know that in 1952 Trueman put India to the sword with fire and slaughter

A CRICKET MATCH AT BRADING, ISLE OF WIGHT

"*Country grounds in some of the loveliest settings . . .*"

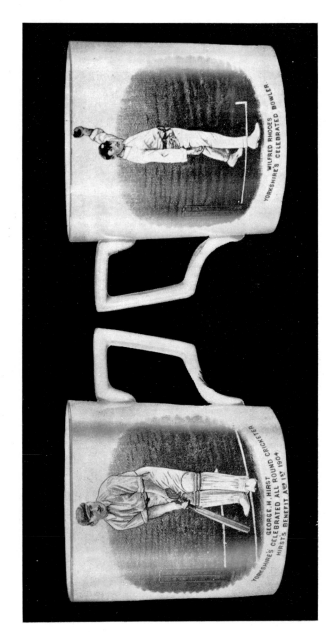

'TWO REAL TYKES' (G. H. HIRST AND W. RHODES)

"*Nothing will convince me that Hirst and Rhodes are not the two greatest all-rounders the game has ever seen . . .*"

and that the following year, having been ' saved ' until the vital Oval match, he took four for 86, besides fielding finely, and played a true part in a true victory. But they will not say a great deal. In Yorkshire they have many ways of killing their favourite children. But not by over-praise.

Frederick Sewards Trueman, born twenty-three years ago at Stainton, near Doncaster, is a product of the wonderfully varied aspects of Yorkshire coaching. In Yorkshire they begin early, even ante-natally. For instance, they try to arrange that your father should be an excellent local cricketer and that your schoolmasters should consider cricket as an important part of your academic education. On leaving school you will play for your village or factory team and, though you may not, as Fred Trueman did, take twenty-five wickets for 37 runs in your first four matches, Headingley is sure to hear of you, because they would rather hear of a promising bowler than a batsman any day of the week. Scotland Yard takes no keener interest in the whereabouts of a missing criminal than do the Yorkshire county authorities in the whereabouts of a promising young bowler.

When Fred Trueman reached the Headingley nets, he came under the quizzical scrutiny of Bill Bowes and Arthur Mitchell, who, following immemorial Yorkshire custom, did not tell him how good he was, but noted, without open disapproval, that he had a good action, a strong frame and a strange liking for the hard work of fast bowling. I remember my step-Uncle Walter's getting angry with somebody who denied the basic intelligence of cricketers.

" Ridiculous," cried my ancient relative. " Most sensible chaps in the world. Though mind you," he added thoughtfully, " I wouldn't exactly say fast bowlers. . . ."

It seems odd that anybody should undergo the rigours of becoming a fast bowler, *and like it*, but that is what Trueman did. He went, when only seventeen, on a southern tour with an eleven of the Yorkshire Federation (virtually a third county team) and did some destructive bowling. In 1949 he had some half a dozen games for the County first eleven; the following

C

year about twice as many. That year, too, he appeared in a Test trial, where he bowled fast and had fun.

There is a pretty story of one of Trueman's early county matches when he was bowling at Oxford against the University. He was hurling them down at great pace when suddenly there was a click as the ball flew away towards fine leg, and Brennan with an acrobatic leap brought off a sensational wicket-keeper's catch. Dazzled by the sheer brilliance of it, Trueman dashed up the pitch, engulfed the astonished stumper in a soccer centre-forward's embrace, and ecstatically exclaimed for all the world to hear: "Well copped, lad!"

For a long time "Well copped, lad," was the most popular catchword in the Oxford Parks.

It was in 1951 that Trueman performed his first act of genuine devastation in a county game, taking eight Notts wickets for 51 and achieving the hat-trick. He took nearly a hundred wickets that year, but the next two seasons saw him performing his National Service in the R.A.F., and this prevented anything more than an occasional appearance for his county. The Service authorities, however, gave him leave to play in Test matches, and in 1952 the touring Indians were indeed butchered to make a Trueman holiday. His Test analysis against India read:

119·4 overs, 25 maidens, 29 wickets, 386 runs: average, 13·31.

In the Manchester game he actually took 8 wickets in as many overs for 31, while in the Indians' second innings at Leeds he was the chief architect of a catastrophe which caused the scoreboard to read: no runs for four wickets; truly the most shattering figures ever registered in a Test match. In 1953 he was, for one reason or another, unable to have sufficient practice early on, and when I saw him at Lord's in the Yorkshire match with Middlesex, he bowled with considerably more enthusiasm than accuracy, and Compton played ducks and drakes with him, as he did with every other bowler that after-noon. Perhaps it is hard on *any* bowler to find Denis Compton on a punishing day. At any rate, there were doubts on that

day as to whether Trueman really was the fast bowler the
selectors had been praying for. There was also a damaged
ankle, which caused pain to its owner, and distress to those who
were anxiously watching his fate. The fairest thing to say is
that for the 1953 season, at least, all was well that ended well.
He did not play for England until the fifth Test, but then,
bowling with rare fire and skilfully nursed by his captain, he did
his duty nobly.

And is he like Larwood? Well, he is of the same stocky, deep-
chested build. He was once a miner and proud of it. He also
runs up with great force, with some detriment to the turf
as he finishes his run. After the Manchester match against
India in which Trueman wrought such havoc, the chairman of
the Old Trafford ground committee shook his head over the
heavy bootmarks and said:

" You know, Fred, it's a good job it's Yorkshire you play for."

" Oh, ay? " said Fred easily.

" They've got plenty of grounds, but we've only one, and if
you mucked it up the same as you've done today, we soon
wouldn't even have that one left."

All the same, they are still putting down no red carpet in
Yorkshire.

" Give the lad another two years," they say. " And then
we'll show 'em. . . ." I like that *we*.

CHAPTER IV

DIGEST OF STATISTICS

I

IT was a Victorian politician who said: " There are lies, thundering lies and statistics. . . ." What a naïve, sentimental, essentially Victorian point of view that was! It suggests a time when the whole human race was not enslaved by statistics. In those days there was at least resistance. Happy time. . . . It would be interesting to speculate on the cause of this declension of the human family and on how such a hideous phenomenon as statistics should have been allowed to run amok in the world. Statistics, considered in a general way, would appear to have been invented for the sole purpose of lowering human morale. It seems a pity.

Now, men and women, in my opinion, were meant by Providence to be men and women. It seems a modest requirement. Yet, once they have been turned into statistics, where are they? In this odd, but interesting, age in which we live we are all fodder for some kind of statistician, whatever his racket may happen to be, whether it be economic, medical, social or something even more repellent. How can anybody feel a proper self-respect if he has been reduced to a mere statistic? Do you know that you are (or quite possibly are not) 0·000022 of the working population of the United Kingdom of Great Britain and Northern Ireland, excluding the Isle of Man, but including the Isle of Dogs? Does your heart beat quicker to discover that you consume 0·00000227 of the 1,062,742,659 gallons of the medicine put away in a week (month or year) under the National Health Service Act of 1946? You ought to be not merely surprised: you should be astounded.

You may be under the illusion that you are a very normal average person with a nice home, a nice wife and three children. But are you? Not to the statistician. He will not in this realistic age allow you such a sentimental bit of nonsense as a home. You are merely the licensed occupier of 0·024 of a statutory accommodation unit (permanent or temporary), excluding houses built by the Scottish Special Housing Association, except in Kincardine, Clackmannan and the Stewartry of Kircudbright. As for your wife, poor wretch, the statistician will not allow you a whole one. All you are permitted, as the average Englishman, is 0·72 of a wife, and you may reckon yourself peculiarly fortunate that he allows you three-quarters of a better half. Your offspring do not, as you fondly suppose, number three, but 2·87. By the time the statistician has finished with you, you will hardly have a rag to your back. Unless my calculations are wrong, you will probably find yourself with no more luxurious wardrobe than 2·35 shirts and 1·87 pairs of trousers.

This rather churlish attack upon the whole gang of statisticians suggests an unreasonable prejudice on my part. I stick to my prejudices, and do not mind being unreasonable. I dislike the statistician, as such, because he takes a friendly, harmless human creature, compounded of flesh and blood, and turns him into a cipher, a fraction, a mere decimal point. But from my strictures on the foul race of statisticians I freely except the cricket statistician, who is a high-minded fellow and comports himself in exactly the opposite manner to his depraved opposite numbers. The common statistician, I say, reduces a man to a figure. The cricket statistician by the power of evocation raises figures into men. He does this as surely as did old Tom Emmett, who, when asked what was his batting average during a bad patch, replied with human passion: " Owt, nowt, blank decimal bloomin' nothing ! "

The cricket statistician is conversant with the happier facts of life. To him the whole of cricket history is treasure trove, an inexhaustible storehouse of drama, character and pageantry. Into the magical lucky dip of his knowledge he can pop in his thumb and pull out a prize or plum, some simple fact or series of facts which, in the light of imagination, can tell a tale, paint a picture, or light a lamp of memory.

Sometimes he will fire a question at you, well knowing (*a*) that you do not know the answer and (*b*) that you know he does. When, for instance, did W. G. Grace keep wicket in a Test match? Absurd. Oh, yes, he did. It was in the third Test at the Oval in 1884, two years after the fatal game which made the Ashes for ever a burning question. The fact is that the Australians won the toss and proceeded to pile up the first Test total of 500 runs, including the first individual score of 200. This came from the bat of Australia's captain, W. L. Murdoch, who topped the double hundred by eleven, and two other batsmen, McDonnell and Scott, also made centuries. It was when the score had reached 500 for six that the English captain decided on desperate measures. He called on his wicket-keeper, the Honourable Alfred Lyttelton, to take the ball, while W. G., who had that day already fielded in every spot from long-on to deep third-man, took over the gloves. Why, the argument seemed to run, shouldn't the wicket-keeper bowl? Everybody else had. The immediate result was as fascinatingly improbable as a school story. With his laughable lobs Lyttelton took four wickets for 19, including one presented to him through a smart catch by his successor behind the stumps. Against the gigantic total of 551 England started ill and fared worse, and eight wickets had fallen for 181 when W. W. Read joined Scotton. Walter Read of Surrey was a fine hitter and hit all the harder, it is said, because he was furious at having been demoted to No. 10; Scotton, on the other hand, was one of the stone-wallers of history. Each played his own game to the top of his bent, Read driving fiercely for 117, and Scotton, who had gone in first with W. G. and seemed to have been there since time immemorial, scored 90 at a snail's pace. As a left-hander, he must have driven the fieldsmen near to madness. Mr. Punch celebrated this feat with a parody of Tennyson's *Break, break, break* which began " Block, block, block . . ." But Scotton's stubbornness undoubtedly saved the game for England. Other famous stone-wallers were Barlow of Lancashire and Louis Hall of Yorkshire.

There are many questions the statistician might ask you. What was the lowest total ever made by England in a Test? The answer is 45, and I hope it will remain the lowest. It was in the first Test played by Arthur Shrewsbury's second (1886–87) touring team at Sydney. It was Turner and Ferris who did the damage, and England did very little better in their second innings. Indeed, when they had lost seven wickets they were only 20 runs ahead. But the last four Englishmen, again including Scotton, fought so obstinately with their backs to the wall that they set Australia 111 to win. It was too many for them—13 too many.

And when, do you suppose, did two English teams tour Australia at the same time? Good gracious! how could such a thing happen? In 1887–88 two did. One was led by Lord Hawke and the other by C. A. Smith. Who was he? He was Round-the-Corner Smith of Cambridge and Sussex, of whom you have probably heard. He was also Sir Aubrey Smith of Hollywood, of whom you have certainly heard. Although there were two teams, for the solitary Test match, they chose one eleven from the two, and under W. W. Read's captaincy, they won a low-scoring match by 126.

Here is an oddity, magnificent in its irrelevance. Australia's first innings in the second Test at the Oval in 1888 was an unlucky tangle of thirteens. Three men scored 13 each, one scored twice 13, and the rest made 13 between them. It happened on the 13th of the month, and perhaps England ought to have won by 13. As a matter of fact England won by an innings and 137.

Let me ask you one more: when did W. G. Grace bag a pair in a Test match? The answer is simple: never. But he was once as near to it as it is possible to be. It was in that fiercely exciting match at the Oval in 1890, which England, after a spectacular collapse, won by two wickets. And the Old Man got a duck in the first innings and had a struggle to make one in the second. It just shows you. . . .

There is, of course, a kind of cricket statistician who spreads himself on the irretrievably irrelevant and whose peculiar researches have been enshrined in the characteristic limerick:

> There was a young fellow named Clover,
> Who bowled forty-five wides in an over,
> Which had never been done
> By an archdeacon's son
> On a Friday in August at Dover.

Some people collect slightly eccentric statistics of this kind. When, for example, did three brothers captain two county teams in the same week? You may argue that it does not matter, but if you think it does, the answer refers to that particularly happy band of brothers, the Gilligans. It was in a particular week in 1920 when A. E. R. ("What do *you* think, Arthur?") and A. H. H. Gilligan captained Sussex in successive matches, while brother Fred (F. W., the wicket-keeper one) captained Essex. A world-shattering occasion. Or was it? What do you think, Arthur?

2

I like the statistician best when he is simple and straight-forward, and when he hands you out a plain fact or two, allowing you to put life into them for yourself. Pick up any old Wisden, be its yellow cover never so shabby, and set this life-giving touch to work. Here are a few figures: ooo. Such figures I recognize at sight. They are, alas, not strangers to me. Set them down vertically for a change:

S. E. Butler c Bourne b Cobden .   .   . o
T. H. Belcher b Cobden   .   .   . o
W. A. Stewart b Cobden   .   .   . o

Nothing palpitating in these small details. Three men have, apparently, got ducks. All good men have joined the noble army of saints and martyrs and got ducks in their day. Hutton once had three in a row. So had Denis Compton. But be patient. The key-word is Cobden; not the nobly whiskered apostle of universal peace through free trade, but F. C. Cobden, the Cobden of Cobden's match, the University game of 1870.

An interesting year, in which the measure introducing 'popular' education was brought to the Statute Book. This game at Lord's must have comprised an education in itself. For Cambridge, Yardley (William not Norman) had, by hard driving to leg, hit exactly 100—the first in university matches—and J. W. Dale, who made 67, was caught on the boundary by C. J. Ottaway, a tall fellow, who took the ball one-handed at his full height above the heads of the spectators. The same Dale, when sternly reproved by his captain for missing an easy catch in Oxford's first innings, gave the classic answer: " Sorry, Walter. I was watching a lady getting out of a drag." Picture that scene and its delightful implications.

If you cannot picture it, get hold of a volume of *Punch* for the period, and see, preferably in drawings by Du Maurier, the ladies, the dresses, the drags. . . .

At the beginning of Cobden's last over, Oxford needed only four runs to win with three wickets to fall. Hill tried to clinch the matter by hitting a swashbuckling four, but the ball was miraculously fielded by A. A. Bourne at mid-off and turned into a mere single. Off the second ball Butler tried the same hell-for-leather death-or-glory stroke. It was death, for Bourne heroically caught him. The third ball bowled Belcher and then, with three runs still needed to win, Stewart came in. He walked with slow step to the wicket and all the air a solemn stillness held. . . . There was indeed a breathless hush. When the fourth ball of Cobden's over bowled Stewart, poor sacrificial victim, neck and crop, there was a silent time-lag of an infinitesimal fraction of a second. Then Lord's went mad, and the casualties among silk hats, hurled into the air and danced on, must have been appalling. Cobden was chaired round the ground.

The odd thing is that, apart from this over, Cobden's bowling had not been world-shaking. E. E. H. Ward, who took six for 30, had bowled far better. Yet Cobden's over is immortal, and who has heard of Ward? It is an unjust world.

More than half a century later a celebrated writer, obsessed from his youth by all that he had heard about Cobden's match, tried hard, and finally managed, to track down one of the very few survivors of the game.

" Tell me, sir," he said, " can you recall Cobden's wonderful over ? "

The old gentleman shook his head.

" To tell you the truth, I never saw it. I couldn't bear the tension. *I shut my eyes. . . .*"

3

Take a glance at another little group of figures:

Hirst not out	58
Rhodes not out.	6

Perhaps you do not at once recognize these figures, though I think a Yorkshireman should. But if I added one line more, *anybody* would recall the scene:

G. L. Jessop c Noble b Armstrong . . 104

There is no difficulty in placing the figures at once. Jessop's match. The Oval, 1902. Probably it is the most dramatic story, certainly the most celebrated, in all cricket history. Everybody knows how when England were left 263 to win, five wickets fell for 48. Then Jessop joined Jackson, and there followed the most thrilling pyrotechnic display that the benevolent Oval gasometers have ever looked down on Then Jackson went, and at last Jessop went, too, in a blaze of glory. When the ninth wicket fell and young Wilfred Rhodes strode out from the pavilion gateway, fifteen runs were still wanted. It is part of history (much history being pure legend) that Hirst said to Rhodes: " We'll get 'em in singles, Wilfred. . . ." Everybody knows, too, that this has been stated to be a mere figment of imagination. The problem has not yet been solved, because when, fifty years later, I asked Hirst whether he actually did say it, he told me: " You don't remember *what* you say at such times. . . ." Get them they did, though not entirely in singles.

The story of Jessop's match has been recalled many times, but I set it down here once more for a particular reason. The game was a triumph for England but, also fifty years later, I have heard of a tragedy, minor but poignant, connected with it. In the summer of 1902 P. G. Wodehouse, the greatest English humorist since Dickens, was a clerk in the Hong Kong and Shanghai Bank On that day he dashed across from the City to the Oval instead of having any lunch, and saw Jackson and Jessop start their stand. He did not even take time to buy a sandwich. Alas, time marches on; indeed, it ' gallops withal ' when Jessop is batting. . . . When Jessop had made 39, poor Wodehouse had to go, for time and tide and the Hong Kong and Shanghai Bank wait for no man. " I always remember," he told me, " how formidable Trumble seemed that day. One got the feeling that he was unplayable. And the wicket was in a horrible state by that time. . . ." Seeing Jessop make 39 out of that immortal 104 and not being there at the most dramatic finish in history must have been like seeing Ellen Terry in the first act of *Romeo and Juliet* and then having to leave the gallery because your nose was bleeding. If that had happened to me, I should never have smiled again. It just shows that a noble spirit cannot be quelled. . . .

Here is a simple statistic, perhaps not so well known:

Jackson b Cotter . . . . . o

Thereby indeed hangs a tale. If I say this refers to *the* Jackson, you must think tolerantly of my age and my original location. I mean no disrespect to the present Derbyshire fast bowler or Leicestershire all-rounder or the ancient Jackson, whose ' pace was very fearful. . . .' For me there will always be one Jackson above all other Jacksons. The Hon. F. S. Jackson did not often get a duck, especially in 1905, that wonderful year of his, when he won the toss five times, headed the batting and bowling averages, and defeated the Australian visitors in the Tests by two wins and the best, or virtually the best, of three draws. But there was no direct promise of this happy ending on the first day of the first Test at Nottingham. He did not have quite the team he would have liked to have, as Hirst had a damaged leg and C. B. Fry a badly crushed finger, but strong substitutes were available and, having won the toss on a Trent Bridge wicket even better than usual, Jackson might well have hoped to sit back in the pavilion while his leading batsmen founded a formidable score.

In the course of the morning he was back in the pavilion all right, but so, too, were Tom Hayward, A. O. Jones, the Notts captain who was substituting for Fry, and the great A. C. Mac-Laren.   Jackson had been clean bowled by ' Tibby ' Cotter, the fastest, if not the best, Australian bowler between Ernest Jones and Lindwall, while the other three had fallen victims to Frank Laver, whose length was as immaculate as Cotter's was erratic.   Nevertheless, although it was Laver who got most of the wickets, it was Cotter who put the fear of sudden death into the batsmen with his high-bouncing deliveries.   One of those who came (and went) later said: " Funny thing, you know, I thought of my wife and children. . . ." Johnnie Tyldesley, however, was playing like the master he was, and, fast as Cotter bowled, Tyldesley cut him to the boundary even faster. Bosanquet, playing in his first Test in England, gave Johnnie some valuable help, and when these two were out, Lilley and Rhodes resisted stubbornly.   But, all in all, it was a sorry show, and before four o'clock, on that perfect wicket, England were all out for 196.   Jackson must have wondered. . . .

It was now Australia's turn to start disastrously.   Duff was out for one to a clever catch by Tom Hayward, and Trumper, after compiling an unlucky thirteen in three fours and a single, ricked his back and had to retire.   After that Hill and Noble hit lustily, and it looked as though a big score was inevitably under way until Jackson, still, I think, smarting from that duck, put himself on to bowl.   It was an over in the Cobden class, and delivered on a more momentous occasion.   Noble was caught at the wicket off the first ball, Hill was beaten and bowled by the fourth, and Darling, the Australian captain, was caught in the slips off the first ball he received.   After an over as destructive as that, the batsmen were glad to call it a day.

Next morning, though Cotter made some savage hits, the innings was quickly polished off, partly by some more fine bowling by Jackson, who in all took five for 52, and partly by some remarkable fielding, particularly by Jessop at cover and Jones in the slips. Nobody has ever bettered Jessop; few—Braund, maybe, or Tunnicliffe—have ever bettered Arthur Jones.

The rest of the game was England's all the way. For the batting, everything went just as right as it had gone wrong the previous day. Everybody made some runs, MacLaren scoring a flawless 140. He did this, not so much in his usual classic style as by powerful, punishing hitting. Jackson, who was 82 not out, robbed himself of an almost certain century by declaring at 426 for five wickets. What was more important was to have the whole of the third afternoon at his disposal for the disposal of the enemy. As it turned out, he did not need the full time. Without the injured Trumper, the unhappy Australians never had a look in. Certainly they never looked like making the 400 necessary runs. Bosanquet completely baffled them, as he had done some fifteen months before at Sydney, when he had been one of P. F. Warner's conquering heroes. On that occasion they had dashed down the pitch and been stumped. At Nottingham those who did not exhibit this recklessness stood their ground and were trapped off the edge. ' Bose ' took eight for 107, and only Gregory had a clue to the problem of dealing with him. This English victory laid the foundation of a sure and fine triumph in the rubber, but I am entitled to the opinion that Jackson was called to the full height of his powers by that unceremonious duck at the hands of Cotter. There is one other odd fact, irrelevant, I think, to every other fact on earth and, therefore, pleasing to the statisticians. It so happens that the two captains in the 1905 rubber, F. S. Jackson and Joe Darling, were born in different hemispheres on exactly the same day, 21st November, 1870. My second favourite statistician calls this coincidence ' quaint '. I had often wondered what the word meant.

4

Very nearly the most significant statistic of our time is simply
this:

T. E. Bailey b Archer   64

The figure does not indicate an enormous score, nor was this
score compiled, as the critics were eager to point out, in a
manner conducive to what is called Brighter Cricket. Barnacle
Bailey, they called him, as if there was something essentially
ridiculous in his holding the fort, come hell and high water,
when the state of the game emphatically demanded that he
should. I am slow to understand the critics' attitude. It is as
though they were abusing Horatius for not dancing a Highland
fling or playing a saxophone solo while he was engaged on the
somewhat more important task of holding the bridge. If
Bailey was a barnacle, he was a barnacle mercifully and im-
movably stuck over a disastrous leak in the English ship.
During the 1953 Tests there were at least three times when,
without such a barnacle, the ship would have been a sheer
hulk. In the second Test at Lord's, Bailey played a paladin's
part in company with the equally gallant Watson. It was very
much the same thing at Leeds, where he filled the breach along
with Laker; at the Oval, in the vital fifth game, his contribution was without doubt on the gold standard. When stumps
were drawn on the Monday evening, England after a good start
had not so much faltered as tottered, and were still 40 runs
behind with only three wickets to fall. But Bailey was there.
In the morning he soon lost Lock, but after that, first with
Trueman and then with Alec Bedser, he rebuilt advantage for
England a brick at a time. It was, to vary the metaphor,
like a tug of war. The battle went first this way and then that;
then, slowly, inch by inch, one side began to assume command
over the other, and England, who might well have finished their
first innings a good many runs behind, led by 31 priceless runs.

Bailey's innings was a signed monograph on courage and
character. He is not a natural stone-waller, but rather a
cheerful and forcing bat if the circumstances allow. His feat

nowhere approached Scotton's o in sixty-seven minutes in 1886. He merely demonstrated that here was his side's sheet-anchor, an invaluable man in a crisis, and, what is more, a genuine all-rounder of the old-fashioned sort.

When victory was finally won, some thousands of happy citizens dashed towards the pavilion to chant: " We want Len. . . ." And Len, that fine sportsman, spoke, as we have seen, not of himself, but of a lot of others, friends and foes who had done honour to the game, not least, Trevor Bailey.

There is no need to write about it. Nearly everybody saw or heard it, everybody read about it at the time. But twenty, thirty, forty, years on it will be nothing more than a statistic, a page reprinted from score-books:

T. E. Bailey b Archer   64

I shall not be there; but when you see it in the old tattered Wisden of 1954 your eyes behind your glasses will light up and your grandchildren will say: " He's off again. . . ."

CHAPTER V

THREE PRINCES CHARMING

I

INDIAN cricketers play for India, and that is right. But before India came into the Test arena, comparatively late in history, there were three Indians who played for England, and played magnificently. The first was the greatest of the three, indeed he was one of the greatest in the history of the game. That phrase ' one of the greatest ' is no mild, conventional compliment, for ' Ranji ' lived in the greatest of cricket periods and was, so far as it is humanly possible to judge, one of the half-dozen greatest players in the game's history, possibly— certainly until the advent of Bradman—one of the three greatest. When he first played for England in 1896 Ranji made 154 not out, but, far more than this splendid score itself, it was the manner of his making it that bemused and enchanted the watching English public, far more magically than anything they had seen before. Lilley, who batted with him in that game, said long afterwards that Ranji's was the most spectacular innings he had ever seen in a quarter of a century's cricket. There was something in his play that changed the whole tone and tenor of the game. Here was one, indeed, " in whose hand the bat became a wizard's wand and orientated afresh the setting of the cricket field."

Each of these three great Indian players made a century on his first appearance for England, but Ranji's century was incomparably the greatest. It is the privilege of the English to maul and manhandle the names of distinguished foreigners, particularly of those whom they most revere. As an abbreviation for Kumar Shri Ranjitsinhji, the disyllable ' Ranji ' was comparatively innocuous. I do not think he could have disliked it, for he had courtesy, kindness and humour. At Cambridge he was called ' Smith ', but to the man on the hard wooden seat he was for ever Ranji. When he became the crowned head of his smallish, but important, Indian state, he was still Ranji to the worshipping crowds from Brighton to Bramall Lane, which is just as well, because what they would have made of Colonel His Highness Shri Sir Ranjitsinhji Vibhaji, Maharaja Jam Sahib of Nawanagar it is difficult to imagine. Ranji was a legend even as Grace and Jessop were legends. He once said that nobody is so soon forgotten as a successful cricketer. In his own person he is a wonderful example of the untruth of this, because it is impossible for him to be forgotten so long as there remains one person, however ancient, who saw him once. Besides, over those who write about cricket (many well and one or two superbly) Ranji, of all cricketers, cast an irresistible spell.

A man who is famous as a cricketer may well wish to be more famous for some other, and weightier, reason, but there was in Ranji nothing of the clown's wistful desire to play Hamlet. He was an aristocrat and knew his duty. He was a statesman and knew his mission. When Ranji and the great Paderewski met at Geneva as representatives of India and Poland, they are reported to have shaken hands and murmured, simultaneously, and with rueful irony: " Aren't you better known for something else? "

But all this was in the nineteen-twenties, a good quarter of a century after the glory and glamour of Ranji the cricketer had burst upon England. He first came to Cambridge in 1891, studying under a private tutor before taking up residence at the University. He played for a scratch Cambridge team called the Cassandra Club, in a manner which it would be an understatement to call unorthodox, and made gargantuan scores on the vast, grassy ocean of Parker's Piece. This was the place where Sir Jack Hobbs first played. Once, they say, Ranji scored a century, slipped away while his side was finishing its innings, wandered across the Piece and, finding a side with a man short, hit up a century in a totally different game, then returned nonchalantly to make a third century in his first team's second knock. If this sounds a tall story, it is a documented fact that some years later he scored two centuries in a day, one before lunch and one after tea, and against Yorkshire.

He was not picked for the University eleven in his first year. This failure to make use of the most remarkable cricketer of the period was due, not to any kind of prejudice against an Indian undergraduate, but to lack of imagination. F. S. Jackson, the Cambridge captain, walking across Parker's Piece one day, came upon an enormous crowd and, stopping to watch, saw, and was unimpressed by, the odd spectacle of a batsman going down on his knees to belt a ball to leg. Jackson, who afterwards became one of Ranji's firmest friends, used to laugh ruefully over his sin of omission. In the meantime Ranji gained an introduction to Fenner's and there was bowled to by relays of professionals, some of them the finest bowlers of the day, who tried to rid him of his worst faults. In practice he was tireless.[1] In trying to teach him to make sound defensive strokes (which he hated) Dan Hayward, the leading professional, took the drastic step of pegging down Ranji's right leg. Thus, as they say, is history born. Instead of playing a defensive shot, as his mentor had intended, Ranji inclined his sinuous body, flicked his supple wrists, and the ball went like a flash to fine leg. Thus the most elegant stroke known to cricket was born under hardship, adversity and a self-imposed handicap. About twenty years later, when he was less slim, less supple and far past his glorious best, I sat as near as I could to the sight-screen behind the bowler's arm at Lord's to watch if I could discover how this historic stroke was made. The bowler, an undeservedly forgotten man named Mignon, was bowling fast, but Ranji's leg glance was quicker—quick enough, it seemed, to deceive the human eye There was that uncanny flick of the wrists and the ball hit the pavilion rails at fine leg like a tracer bullet. He did not appear to have hit it hard; it was almost as if he had struck a match on it as it went by. It was not a chancy deflection or a sneaky ' tickling round the corner '.

[1] C. B. Fry told me that one February day at Cambridge he saw Ranji, in fur gloves, bat two hours before, and two after, lunch to four first class bowlers.

The full blade of the bat met the ball every time. It happened again and again. I was dazzled. I still am.

It now seems incredible that Ranji might never have got his Blue at all if Jackson had not gone to India with a team of amateurs under Lord Hawke's captaincy, and there he saw the light. Indian cricketers, he discovered for the first time, could be brilliant. Next year (1893) Ranji was awarded his Blue, and although he made only 9 and 0 in the Varsity match he played with great success for the Gentlemen against the Players and turned out three times against the Australians.

Stories about Ranji's fielding are apt to approach the lyrical, and the legend that he once caught a swallow in the slips takes a little ' swallowing ', but of the conjuring quality of his fielding there is no doubt. The ball went to him as though drawn by a magnet. In the Varsity's match with Yorkshire that year Tunnicliffe hit a screaming drive into the long field where Ranji was standing. The batsmen started running, the other fieldsmen gaped and Jackson, the captain, shouted: " Don't stand there, Smith; run after it! " It was at this instant that Ranji, with an air of innocent surprise, brought the ball out of his pocket.

Down from Cambridge, Ranji spent most of the next season in Brighton, where began his connection with Sussex, though he did not play for the county till the following year, and his lifelong friendship with C. B. Fry. (They must have met in the 1893 Varsity match when Fry made 31 out of a disastrous 64 in Oxford's second innings.) Ranji also played some matches for the M.C.C., and in a game (ironically against Cambridge University) he celebrated his first meeting with W. G. by sharing a partnership with him of 200 runs in a couple of hours. The fieldsmen suffered the punishment of leather-hunting. In this more humane age fielders are seldom subjected to it.

The floodgates of his popularity were now opened. Against Lancashire he astonished the crowd by glancing their furious fast bowler Mold time and time again ' off his eyebrows '. The Old Trafford spectators, though they like to see Lancashire win, are genuine patrons of art. They know a good thing when they see one. It was in 1896 that Ranji performed his 'impossible' feat of scoring two centuries in one day at Brighton against Yorkshire. It was Douglas Jardine, that tough campaigner and shrewd assessor of cricket values, who, in appraising a player's merits, would demand: "What did he do against Yorkshire?" So perhaps it is not so odd that the very greatest cricketers have reserved their best for Yorkshire bowling: Grace, Fry, Ranji, Hobbs, Hammond—they all did it, as though they revelled in a fight with foemen worthy of their highly tempered steel. This was Ranji's year: the year of his first Test match, in which he made 62 (only one other batsman doing anything at all) and 154 not out, remembered by those who saw it as one of the most dazzling feats ever seen at Old Trafford or anywhere else. This was the year in which his well-beloved picture became fixed in the public mind: the slim, incredibly supple figure with the dark, smiling face; the fluttering silken sleeves, the apparent absence of concentration when the concentration must have been terrific; the faint suggestion that the whole thing was fantasy and that this bizarre prestidigitator would suddenly vanish in smoke on a magic matting, floating high over the Pavilion dome, from Brighton to Baghdad. Sober journalists found in him " an Oriental calm with an Occidental quickness, the stillness of the panther with the suddenness of its spring ". And C. B. Fry, who knew him better than anyone else, said of him: "He moved as if he had no bones: one would not be surprised to see brown curves burning in the grass where one of his cuts had travelled, or blue flame shimmering round his bat as he made one of his leg strokes."

There can never have been eyesight like his. (" Tell me, Ranji, what would you do with a googly? " " I should watch the seams of the ball.")

It was said that so remarkable was his eyesight, he could have gone in against the fastest bowling and scored a century with a rolled umbrella. In Denis Compton's golden year of 1947 I have seen him more than once bat after this glittering fashion and in the Middlesex v. Surrey match at the Oval in 1953 I saw

Compton reduce to impotence the bowlers who had defeated the Australians and won their county the championship. But Compton's brilliance does not glitter every day. Ranji's did. It was by a ghastly irony of fate that in 1915 he was to lose one of those wonderful eyes in a shooting accident. No Grand Guignol dramatist could have invented a crueller *dénouement*.

In the 1896 Gentlemen *v.* Players match he was out after ten minutes, a rare experience for him, but his batting during that short period was of a quality even rarer. In all, he received only thirteen balls. Off the first over (five balls) from Tom Richardson, bowling at his fastest, Ranji hit eighteen runs. When, after a single by his partner, he found himself at the other end, he set about the other bowler, who happened to be Johnny Briggs, of all people. But Ranji was no respecter of persons. In nearly the shortest possible time he raised his score to 47. Off the thirteenth ball received he was out leg before wicket to a delivery which hit him in the stomach. Somebody, either Ranji, Johnny Briggs, or the umpire, must by that time have been growing tired.

In 1897 Ranji wrote, and dedicated to the great Queen, his *Jubilee Book of Cricket*, one of the classics of the game. This book was mainly written while its author lay on a sick bed, where he had been confined with congestion of the lungs. In the same year, once he had recovered from his illness, he played as brilliantly as ever and was fifth in the English batting averages, with nearly 2,000 runs.

So the flood of runs—and popularity—went on and his aggregates were tremendous, by any standard. But he was loved, not because of his mighty scores, but for something which mattered a great deal more; he was loved by his many friends because he was personally charming, piquantly amusing and, above all, wildly generous. (His notorious extravagance sprang mainly from an inability to set a reasonable limit to generosity and hospitality.) He was loved by the crowd because he stood in their eyes for something romantic and fabulous, something 'out of this world' or, at the very least, out of their world. When the statue of Edward the Black Prince

was erected in the City Square at Leeds, one honest partisan
was heard to say: " If Lord Hawke doesn't mind 'em putting
up Ranji, why should I ? " Ranji himself, for obvious reasons,
hated being called the Black Prince. There is in the minds of
the simpler English (may heaven bless every one of them) an
incurably romantic picture of an Eastern potentate, turbaned,
inscrutable, gleaming in silks and jewels, against a background
of gorgeously clad elephants and gorgeously unclad dancing
girls. The Rajah, they call him. The fact that this picture is
pure fantasy does not make it any the less real in their happy
fancy. If the crowd had been told that Ranji would only use a
bat with a diamond splice they would have believed it im-
plicitly. For friends and spectators alike there was magic in
the man.

He was careless with money; he was prodigal with runs.
He behaved as though he could afford to be extravagant with
either. Anybody, provided he is only rich enough, can despise
money, and a cricketer who is truly great can neglect aggregates
and averages. But it is always worth examining the figures of
the man who treats figures with contempt. In all matches
Ranji scored 72 centuries and twice (1899 and 1900) he topped
3,000 in a season. Only Hammond, Hendren and Sutcliffe
have beaten this record and only Hayward and Mead have
equalled it. (Hobbs, Hutton and Compton have scored 3,000
runs only once and Grace never quite managed it, though in
1871, when there were no boundaries and you had to run out
every hit, he scored 2,739.) Ranji took part in the record score
for the seventh wicket: 344 with W. Newham against Essex
at Leyton in 1902. He made over 150 in his first Test in
England and over 170 in his first Test in Australia. His figures
might have been those of a run-piling average-seeker, whereas
every innings he played was a source of fascination and shining
delight.

His subsequent work at the League of Nations and as head of
his own state of Nawanagar are not for a simple cricket book;
yet they are all of a piece with the man: he was a natural federa-
tionist, and took pleasure in bringing opposite interests together;

he was chosen as Chancellor of the Chamber of Indian Princes, though his territory was small, and it is at least arguable that, had he been listened to, the world might have been a more sensible place. As a statesman he invariably took the long view, because he foresaw coming events before other people did; as an individual ruler he was both a liberal and a bene-volent autocrat, perhaps the only genuinely benevolent autocrat who has ever existed.

When he died in 1933, a wider world than the world of cricket was stricken with grief. " He was the first Indian," it was said of him, " who touched the imagination of the British people as a whole, and for that reason it may be said of him that few men did more to bring about a sympathetic under-standing between East and West."

It may well be that men colour with their own sentimental imagination the heroes of their boyhood. It may also well be that these paladins are to the unprejudiced eye mere ordinary men. To err, and to romanticize, is human. But this is simply not true for those of us who were boys and worshipped Ranji. However far the figures of other heroes may recede into forgetfulness, Ranji will be freshly remembered. Ranji was unique.

2

Ranji began his career under the handicap of an English lack of imagination which could not conceive the notion of an Indian as a cricketer. Ranji's brilliant nephew, K. S. Duleep-sinhji, suffered a handicap even more difficult to surmount, for he had to work out his own salvation under the shadow of his almost impossibly brilliant uncle. It was a hard row to hoe. In a sense every fine young cricketer follows a master, as Hobbs followed Hayward and Hutton followed Sutcliffe. But this relationship was both simpler and subtler. Here was a clever young man, whose very stance at the crease challenged com-parison with his illustrious uncle. Yet the very burden of the comparison was a heavy one for young shoulders.

Kumar Shri Duleepsinhji was born in 1905 at Sarador, a

village in his uncle's state of Nawanagar, and Ranji, as his guardian, sent him to school at Cheltenham. Even before ' Duleep ' set off on the voyage to England his cricket education had begun. Personal coaching by Ranji, who had now succeeded to the headship of his state, started when Duleep was eight years old. One of the reasons why Duleep was able to come to England at all was that the Jam Sahib had, by his own skill and careful rule, restored his state's finances. While he was at Cheltenham his guardians were Beatrice and C. B. Fry, and there can never have been better guardians than that remarkable pair, whether for cricket or character. In their work for the training ship *Mercury* they must have wielded a strong influence over the lives of many hundreds of lads, who were like King Arthur's knights, ' some good, some bad, but all stamped with the image. . . .' Duleepsinhji's reputation as a schoolboy, indeed as a man, was as the perfection of good manners in that period of the nineteen-twenties when the young, whatever their other virtues, were not crippled by courtesy. His was not the outlook of the beefy he-man. He was noticeably kind to waiters and he did not disdain an evening at the ballet. This rash incursion into æsthetics, though it may have puzzled his simpler-minded friends, did not prevent him from starting off well as a cricketer at Cambridge. There was no chance of his being neglected because he was an Indian, and his success at the University was far greater than Ranji's. His average in his first year was nearly 50 and in his second year just under 40. All the time he was immensely popular. He was also happy until attacked by a bout of pneumonia, an illness which must be a continuing menace to the Indian who exchanges his coral strand for a climate that is ' sodden and unkind '. This put him out of cricket for a longish period in 1927. In 1928, however, he recovered, came back, and made five centuries.

And now he was fulfilling his ambition to play regularly for Sussex, his uncle's old county. In 1929 he did something which was rather unusual in one of his modest nature. In the return match against Kent he made 246 not out. Now there was nothing unexpected about this big score, even its excellence, for he was at the time in glorious form; what was remarkable was that after the first Kent match he had bet Lord Harris he would make a double century in the second. In all, 49 centuries, including several double ones, came from his bat, but this is the only recorded instance of a boast. I do not know the size of the bet—it was probably half-a-crown—but I think Lord Harris must have paid up with a sense of rueful pleasure. In the same year Duleep ' christened ' the new scoreboard on the Hove ground by a score of 333 against Northants. This was a stupendous achievement and has remained the highest score ever made by a batsman in the county of those prolific scorers, Fry and Ranji. And he made it in one day.

In 1930 he played in his first Test match for England. Ranji went to Lord's and watched every ball of it. " I am the proudest man in England," he said to a friend (but not to Duleep) when Duleep made 173. " I have realized one of my greatest ambitions, and am basking in reflected glory. . . ." One of the most difficult relationships in the world is that between a father and son, or an uncle and nephew who are almost father and son, for the one sometimes proudly and affectionately demands far more than the other can give him. Duleepsinhji, normally the most light-hearted and charming of companions, was playing under a strain when his uncle was watching him, while Ranji's affection was so anxious and his standards so almost impossibly high, that it was a long time before he permitted his nephew to know how good he thought him. . . . Duleep worshipped Ranji, and Ranji sternly masked the pride that he felt in the younger man's achievements. Duleep would have given his right hand to feel that he had deserved the great man's praise. Legend has preserved (or invented) a whole string of messages sent from uncle to nephew.

" Why did you get out at 187? A man ought to score his first hundred for his side, but he should not then rest content; he ought to get the *second* hundred for his side. With the third hundred you may have fun on your own account. . . ."

And there was the alleged telegram that arrived after a poor score in a Test: " *Go and play tennis with Betty Nuttall* ".   (This was nothing to the telegram that arrived simultaneously for the team's captain.)   But Ranjitsinhji's unrelenting criticism came from an exaggerated sense of responsibility.   In imagination he played every ball that Duleep received.   Every time Duleep was out, Ranji imagined himself walking back to the pavilion. And by the same token, he must have thrilled with delight when Duleep made an elegant century, one of them not out, in each innings of the Gentlemen *v.* Players match.   (Only R. E. Foster and King of Leicestershire had ever done that.) He was to make another in the 1932 match.

In 1931 Duleep was on top of the world.   He was one of the cricketers—almost certainly *the* cricketer of the year.   His four successive centuries were a delight to the eye, either of the technician or the æsthete.   When he captained Sussex, the spirit of the team was one of supreme confidence and loyalty. There was in the side a strong will to win, and the attractive cricket which the players produced drew life and colour from the attractive personality of their captain, which made itself felt from No. 2 to No. 11.   Sussex cricket enjoyed one of its happiest periods.

In 1932 came tragedy.   Sussex had had a splendid season. In their last championship match, at a vital point of the season, Duleep broke down.   His doctor did not wish him to play, but Duleep had the strongest feeling that his uncle wished him to turn out and do his best.   In the game he made 93, playing one of the best innings of his life.   Immediately afterwards he collapsed in the pavilion, and has never played since.   It was a personal tragedy for the man himself.   He had played for England, but his breakdown prevented him from ever playing for India.   That was a tragedy for Indian cricket.

Yet this graceful and gracious person survived tragedy. The Jam Sahib died in 1933, and that old India, in which he had played so honourable and statesmanlike a part, within the next fifteen years died too.   Much that was splendid went; but the new India lived and lives.   When the new Government of India came to power, Duleepsinhji became a private citizen.

On certain tours he served Indian cricket as a journalist. Now he has gone further. As Ranji faithfully served the old India, so Duleep serves the new India. As the High Commissioner for India in Australia, that mighty member of the cricket Commonwealth, he spent a happy period, living and working among people who understand him and whom he understood. The new India cannot have a more faithful servant.

3

Three is the perfect number, and the third great Indian cricketer who played for England was the Nawab of Pataudi. He did not come as an unheralded genius like Ranji, or as the heralded protégé of a genius like Duleep, yet his career followed a close parallel with theirs and, because he played a little later, he did what neither of them ever did: that is, he played both for England and India. Like his predecessors, he scored a century in his first Test for England; like them, he also scored a century in the Gentlemen v. Players match. His record in University matches is not merely more remarkable than that of his fellow Indians; it is more remarkable than that of anybody else at all. He came to England at the age of sixteen, after receiving excellent coaching at his school in Lahore, and, before going up to Oxford, he was lucky enough to undergo further tuition at the hands of the great Frank Woolley. This was in itself as distinguished a tutelage as learning singing from Melba.

He did not get a Blue in his first year, but in 1929, after a moderate success in the ordinary games, he burst into full flower in the University match with a century in the first innings and 84 in the second. I have said ' burst into flower '; it would have been equally fair to say ' burst into flame ', for his batting had about it, besides polished elegance, a kind of devouring fire. In the following year he did not achieve much, but in 1931 he attacked the bowling of all the opposing teams with impartial fury and, before the Cambridge match, scored four centuries in a row. At one point in the season he had made 654 runs for only four times out. But his feat in the University match was more memorable than anything in the history of that series. Until the first day of this game the record score in the Oxford *v.* Cambridge encounters had stood at 172 not out, scored by J. E. Marsh for Cambridge in 1904. Batting on the first day of the 1931 match, A. T. Ratcliffe of Cambridge broke his record by compiling a valuable, if stolid, total of 201. It was rather hard on Ratcliffe, an excellent player and a good sportsman, that Pataudi should have registered a determination to surpass that score, or perish in the attempt. Marsh's record had lasted for twenty-seven years. Ratcliffe's was beaten in a day. For beaten it was, Pataudi going on to make 238 not out, amid applause more tumultuous than had been heard in a university game since Cobden's match. This score remains, and seems likely to remain, an Oxford *v.* Cambridge record. Pataudi also came near to perishing in this successful attempt, for so tremendous was the nervous tension to which he subjected himself that when reaching the pavilion he collapsed.

Like Duleepsinhji, he was never robust; he did not enjoy complete freedom from illness, either in England or in Australia, where he toured with Jardine's winning team in 1932–33, making in the first Test at Sydney a vigorous century which contributed largely to England's victory.

Back in England, ill-health handicapped him at frequent intervals and he was not able to play regularly. When, however, he was well enough to turn out, he played for Worcestershire, and made some excellent scores. I never saw Pataudi and C. F. Walters playing together, though I have watched each of them with delight on separate occasions, and would place both high up on my list of charmers. When they were batting together for Worcestershire, the play must have been worth travelling many a long mile to see. After Pataudi had practically dropped out of the game in the 'thirties he was not seen on the cricket-field until ten years later, when he toured England with the Indian side of 1946, the first visitors to come here after the war. Then, although he had some rewarding knocks in county matches, he did little or nothing in the Tests.

Like some others in the same position, when India became

ndependent Pataudi found himself without a state to rule. Although a Moslem, he threw in his lot with the new India, and joined the staff of the Indian Foreign Office. He was incapable of doing anything half-heartedly, and it was characteristic of his indomitable will-power that he died of a heart attack after taking part in a fierce polo match. It is obvious that he should not have played that game of polo. But, just like Duleepsinhji, he never avoided risk or danger and, in the end, danger took him. He left a boy, now twelve years old, who is going to be a fine cricketer. For his father's sake he deserves success.

4

In the roll of cricketing merit those three great Indians are likely to be set down in the order in which I have given them. Ranji, first; Duleep, second and Pataudi a good third. This can be said without disrespect to the second and third, for Ranji was a wizard, a magician, who, had he played in the Middle Ages, might have been denounced by bowlers as having traffic with the Evil One. After a long inquisition by a mediæval M.C.C., he might well have been burnt at the stake. In any team of all climes and all ages Ranji would automatically find a place; I cannot think of anyone who ever saw him who would deny him such a place. By comparison with this luminous figure, Duleepsinhji is to be reckoned a little lower than the angels, and Pataudi a little lower still, but still only a little lower. They were like three boys at the top of the form's examination list with marks of 100, 95 and 90 per cent. Even then, I should want to give Ranji 110 per cent.

Their frames were delicate, but each one had a will which, like his wrist, was of steel. All three suffered from frequent bouts of illness; all three played under this cruel handicap, and not merely played, but played with sparkle, brilliance and vivid virility. All three, among all but their greatest contemporaries, were as Arab barbs among heavy hunters—I will not say dray-horses, for there were few of these, at least in Ranji's time. All three had that attribute which belongs to

none but the very best: the appearance of having any amount
of time for every stroke, even off the fastest bowling; furthermore, you must remember that, while Duleep and Pataudi
played against Larwood, Ranji played against Mold, Lockwood,
Richardson, Kortright and Brearley. Pataudi's footwork was
wonderfully quick; Duleep's was quicker; Ranji's was uncanny. Pataudi fell short by a hair's breadth of that perfection
of supple grace which was the glory of the other two, but after
playing himself in, he could hammer the bowlers, without
appearing to employ brute strength, until they almost cried for
mercy. It was a great privilege to have seen any of them play.

The East has received many a gift from the West, for which
the East has not always been grateful. For the gift of the East
of Ranji, Duleep and Pataudi the West is eternally grateful.

CHAPTER VI

STUMPERS OF THE WORLD, UNITE

I

I HAVE always been interested in wicket-keepers, if only to the extent of wondering why any particular character should be such a glutton for punishment. Life is hard enough as it is, and makes an Aunt Sally of a man often enough in the ordinary way without his having to submit to voluntary Aunt Sallyism six days a week or even Saturday afternoons. Why do men volunteer for forlorn hopes? Why do they rush to become paratroopers, frogmen or operators of midget submarines? It may be that their motives are as mixed and various as those who volunteer for pensionable jobs at the age of sixteen. I volunteered myself for the job of wicket-keeping as a small boy, partly because I was too erratic to be a good bowler and too nervous to be a good bat; and partly because the initials of my Christian names were the same as those of the greatest wicket-keeper of the day. One summer holiday I secured a whole fortnight's cricket on the sands by telling the other boys that this great man was my uncle. It was a shocking thing to do, particularly as my mendacity was accepted by my playfellows without suspicion or question. My conscience, a most un-reliable organ, did not succeed in forcing me to confess my sin, but it did oblige me to go through the motions of keeping wicket with a kind of dedicated passion. All through that happy fortnight I would volunteer to keep wicket for both sides in our pick-up games, and every day I would crouch intently behind the stumps, the world forgetting, until tide stopped play.

I never thought much about the knocks I suffered at school—they were part of the price I had to pay for getting into the eleven three years before my time—but I have often wondered how the earliest wicket-keepers resigned themselves to so much suffering.   The prophets of Baal who cut and gashed themselves with knives in masochistic fury were sensible, even phlegmatic characters compared with the self-immolating souls who first took up wicket-keeping.

Who was the first of these pioneers?   There may have been earlier ones than Tom Sueter, of Hambledon, but none has been described in such majestic phrase.   The words of Nyren have an almost biblical quality:

> 'What a handful of steel-hearted soldiers are in an important pass, such was Tom keeping wicket.   Nothing went by him, and for coolness and nerve in this trying and responsible post, I never saw his equal.   As a proof of his quickness and skill, I have numberless times seen him stump a man out with Brett's tremendous bowling."

And you must remember that " Brett was, beyond all comparison, the fastest, as well as the straightest, bowler that was ever known. . . ."   At the time.

2

The wicket-keeper of Tom Sueter's day was a knight without armour, a paladin without panoply.   He held this ' trying and responsible post ' without pads or gloves, the former of which had not been heard of.   He also adopted an upright stance, as different as possible from the monkey-like crouch which is almost universal to-day.   " The position of the wicket-keeper in his standing," says *The Young Cricketer's Tutor*, " should be that of a man preparing to spar. . . ."   Nyren's later advice to the young wicket-keeper was sound for any age:

> "The wicket-keeper should also stand a little distance behind the wicket, yet not so far back that he may, by a short and quick step, stump out the batter, should he move from his ground.   My reason for recommending that he should remove a little backward from the wicket is because by his doing so the catches will be more easy and he may stump as well. . . ."

Nyren also came down heavily on the side of the quiet, unobtrusive wicket-keeper, and did not hesitate to express his scorn of the fussy one.   (He would obviously have been a sincere admirer of W. A. Oldfield.)

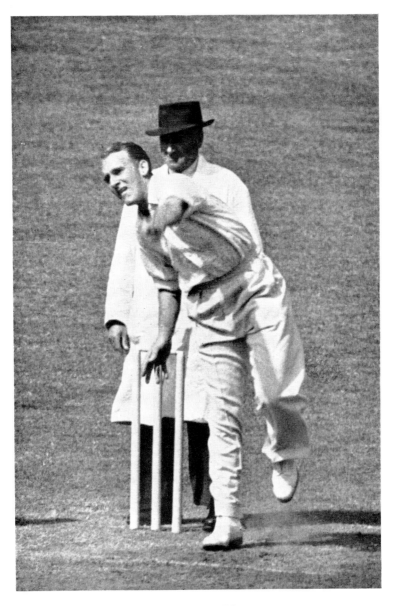

J. H. WARDLE

" He is that rare thing in any walk of life, a genuine humorist . . ."

V. MANKAD

" His hitting was free, swift and vigorous . . ."

"Many wicket-keepers will frequently put down the wicket when the striker has not moved from his ground; but this practice is doubly objectionable in the eyes of a good cricketer, and is after all but a piece of stage effect, and to make a show. . . ."

The first of the great amateur wicket-keepers was Herbert Jenner, later known as Jenner-Fust. The most remarkable fact about him was that the years of his life almost completely spanned the nineteenth century. You would hardly expect wicket-keepers, considering the hard knocks to which they are constantly subjected, to be a long-lived race. Yet Herbert Jenner, who was born in the year after Trafalgar, was alive at the turn of the century and died in the year when P. F. Warner and his team brought the Ashes back from Australia. Well within my own lifetime a book was published which described a contemporary interview with this 'oldest living cricketer', and that he was, at the age of ninety, in full possession of his faculties, his meeting with 'Old Ebor', the prince of interviewers, leaves no doubt. He played for Eton in his time, but this was of necessity some time later than the year (1805) in which Lord Byron played for Harrow. Jenner also took part in the first University match of 1827, making top score for the defeated Cambridge side. (He made 47, while nobody else reached double figures.)

In the great days of his wicket-keeping he played for Kent. His method was to stand a little behind the wicket and to take the ball on either side. Apparently he often stumped a batsman off a ball flying away to leg; perhaps batsmen were bolder in those days than they are now. In any event, he never wore pads and seldom wore gloves. The player of those days would have raised a shout of laughter if he had tried to protect his shins by artificial means, just as Patsy Hendren got a big laugh when, during one of the periodic controversies about 'bumpers', he appeared at the wicket in a crash helmet. But the difference would have been this: Patsy was greeted with happy laughter as an incorrigible joker; the wearer of pads in 1820 would have been greeted with derision as an effeminate creature. I do not know who was the first wicket-keeper to

D

wear pads, though I know who was the first batsman. This
was Robinson—not Emmott Robinson, heaven knows—but
old Bob, one of the Hambledon Robinsons. He was of an
inventive turn of mind and he designed a pair of leg-guards
which were, in effect, thin wooden boards set at an angle.
When the ball hit them they emitted a kind of hollow roar
which sent the Hambledon supporters off into fits of derisory
laughter and old Bob decided that he would be lacerated less
by the flying ball than by the mockery of his comrades. He
discarded his wooden armour, and it was not until round
about 1836 that the parent of the present-day pad was invented
(or re-invented) by an ingenious gentleman in Oxford.

Gloves of a kind had been evolved some ten years earlier,
but these were tubular contraptions for the benefit of the batsman. Nobody cared whether the wicket-keeper lived or died.
Herbert Jenner occasionally wore gloves, but these were not
padded and had no protective purpose; he merely wore light
kid gloves, as a goalkeeper might, to prevent a greasy ball from
slipping out of his hands in wet weather. Grounds were rough
and dangerous, but so skilled was Jenner in 'taking' that he
was never seriously damaged. "The worst I received," he
said with modest pride, " was a fracture of the middle finger of
the right hand and the dislocation of the forefinger."

He used to keep wicket for West Kent to the bowling of that
more than life-size character, the 'kind and manly' Alfred
Mynn, who made the ball 'hum' through the air, and he did
this ungloved, unpadded and, to his eternal credit, with his
withers unwrung. Mynn, whose weight and strength were
colossal, must have been even more 'tremendous' in his
bowling than the semi-legendary Brett, and, when you were
keeping wicket to him on a bumpy pitch, he must have seemed
more manly than kind. He once bowled a ball so fast that it
hit 'second stop' on the chest, and sent him home where he
spat blood for a fortnight.

I cannot leave contemplation of Herbert Jenner without a
feeling of awe: he lived from the reign of George III, through
those of George IV, William IV and Queen Victoria, and into

the reign of Edward VII. He was President of the M.C.C. in
1833 and he retired from cricket twelve years *before W. G. Grace
was born*. And it is a queer fact, though of no interest to anyone but myself, that he was the same age at the time of Waterloo
as I was when he died.

The two wicket-keepers of whom Herbert Jenner thought
highly were E. G. Wenman and old Tom Box. Wenman was
the more reliable of the two, apparently, because Box had a
stiff stance and could not get to a wide ball quickly enough.
I fancy old Tom would have blinked to see Godfrey Evans in
full lateral flight.

One of the most famous wicket-keepers of the early ' middle
period ' was Ted Pooley of Surrey, who was as different from
Herbert Jenner as Sam Weller was from Mr. Pickwick. (What
a Mr. Wardle would Alfred Mynn have made!) Pooley first
handled a bat as a lad on Richmond Green, backing himself in
single-wicket matches for half a crown a time. Like so many
wicket-keepers, he was persuaded early on to try his hand at
bowling. He made a few runs and thought well of himself as a
long-stop but, as for bowling, " Lor' bless yer, guv'nor," said he,
" I had never bowled a ball in a match. I almost laugh now
to think of it. . . ." He got the stumping job because the
hands of the regular Surrey wicket-keeper Lockyer (another old
Tom) were so bruised owing to the fiery surface of the Oval
wicket that he could not take his proper place. Pooley put on
the gloves—it seems they were using gloves by 1863—caught
one and stumped one as to the manner born, and was accepted
by old Lockyer as his successor.

A regular London cock-sparrow of a man, Pooley must have
been physically as hard as nails; violent knocks meant virtually
nothing to him. While Herbert Jenner's hands at ninety were
almost perfect, Pooley's at no more than sixty were knotted and
gnarled like tree-roots. Every finger had been broken at some
time or other and he looked far more like a retired prize-
fighter than an old cricketer. Indeed, he humorously boasted
that after having three teeth knocked out while wicket-keeping
at Lord's—in those days a far wickeder pitch than the Oval—

he received a formal call in the pavilion from a gentleman who
turned out to be, of all people, the great Jem Mace. " Pooley,"
said Mace, " I would rather stand up against any man in
England for an hour than take your place behind the wicket
for five minutes. That ball hit you as if it had struck a brick
wall."

Quite apart from the damage that the bowler may do to him
in the line of duty, it has always seemed to me that a wicket-
keeper takes his life in his hands when keeping wicket behind a
good (or a very bad) hitter. He is always at the mercy of a
violent swing with the bat. It is only a few years ago that
Cyril Washbrook, the Lancashire and England opener, taking a
terrific swing at a loose leg-ball, caught ' Paddy ' Corrall, the
Leicestershire wicket-keeper, on the side of the head. Corrall
received a dangerous concussion, much to the distress of Washbrook, an essentially kindly and sensitive person. And, as
Corrall might have said, parodying a noted wartime wisecrack,
it was no Bank Holiday for him either. Happily he made a
good recovery in time and has spent some seasons on the list of
first-class umpires.

Pooley received a similar blow during a match in Jersey.
Willsher, one of the most famous of the old fast bowlers, was
bowling to a happy islander who, said Pooley, had as much
idea of batting as a crossing-sweeper with his broom. Down
came a ball wide on the leg, the batsman made a mighty
swing, like Umslopogaas whirling his battle-axe, and the next
thing Pooley remembered was lying on the ground and feeling
the doctor grating the bones of his broken nose. . . .

Pooley was the hero, or unwitting villain, of the episode in
New Zealand which deprived England of her regular wicket-
keeper in the very first Test match played against Australia in
1877. You will recollect that, after incredible adventures by
flood and fire, Lillywhite's touring team had arrived at Christchurch to play the local Twenty-Two without sleep and without
even a proper breakfast. (This was the time when Happy Jack
Ulyett made the notorious oven-bottom cakes.) The tourists
performed so badly in the field that heavy bets were taken

against them in the evening of the first day, and this was where poor Ted Pooley found himself in deep waters. The next day England, following Ulyett's champagne supper and a welcome night's rest, proceeded to tan the hides of the local players, and the gentleman who had bet Pooley that the tourists would lose refused to pay up. There was naturally a bit of an argument, followed by a somewhat indiscriminate swinging of fists. I have no doubt that the local gentleman started the *émeute*, but Pooley was detained, and his friends had to go off to Australia without him. England might not have lost that very first Test match if they had had their regular wicket-keeper. (Harry Jupp, the Surrey batsman, had to do the job instead.) Eventually Pooley was put on trial, and when he was acquitted, as he was bound to be, the local people were delighted; so great was their pleasure that they made a collection for him and sent him on his way rejoicing, with £50 and a presentation watch. When he joined his comrades, however, the first Test match had been played and lost. Pooley was a cheery, chirpy, cheeky soul who was always in hot, or at any rate warm, water and finished in what are euphemistically called ' unfortunate circumstances '. He actually read his obituary notice, but as he was in a London workhouse at the time, the news did not cheer him quite as much as it might have done.

From the standpoint of the economic interpretation of history, cricket can have brought little comfort to the old type of professional. Unless he happened to be what is now called a managerial type, like William Clarke or the Lillywhite who took the 1876–77 team to Australia, he was apt to finish a wholly honourable career with very little in his pocket. He was often said to have gone to the devil through drink when, in fact, he had never at any time had enough money to buy more than the odd glass of beer. Those to-day who are liable to think of Lord Hawke or Lord Harris as reactionary, tyrannical old gentlemen are completely ignorant of what they, the former in the north and the latter generally, did to raise the status, social and economic, of the professional cricketer. Those ancient cricketers who are still alive and old enough to remember the bad old days are discriminatingly lavish in their praise of their lordships. Just let anyone try speaking ill of Lord Hawke to an old Yorkshire pro. He will hear something to his disadvantage. The number of professional cricketers who now die in ' un-fortunate circumstances ' is extremely small. This represents a truly genuine improvement, though few I imagine would be as difficult to help as poor Ted Pooley.

Whatever may have been Pooley's shortcomings, it is a fact that in the books he ties with so eminent a person as Don Tallon for the largest number of victims (twelve) in one match.

The name of Pooley suggests Pilling of Lancashire, and Pilling suggests Pinder of Yorkshire. The three Ps. Few would have ventured, apart from local patriotism, to say which was the best of these three. They were all very good indeed. Pilling, whose fame was known far beyond the bounds of Old Trafford, has been called the best keeper before Blackham.

George Pinder was, like George Ulyett, a Sheffield lad, and at the age of ten he was apprenticed to the trade of grinding pocket-knives. He started cricket at eighteen, mainly as a bowler, and began keeping wicket, as a kind of involuntary volunteer, because the regular stumper of his club had not turned up. Soon afterwards he was asked to keep wicket for the local Twenty-Two against an All-England XI. In this game he caught three and stumped two, and before long he was playing, not against, but *for* George Parr's England XI, the youngest among them. His baptism of fire was as fiery as could be. At one end was ' Tear 'em ' Tarrant and at the other the famous, even notorious Jackson of Notts, hero of the contemporary Punch cartoon (29th August 1863), in which the bandaged victim was depicted as exclaiming boastfully: " I've just 'ad a hover from Jackson : the first ball 'it me on the 'and ; the second 'ad me on the knee, the third was in my eye ; and the fourth bowled me out ! " (The caption says: " Jolly game ! ")

But Pinder was a husky fellow with a reach so long that he could take balls wide on either the off or the leg side without shifting his stance When he came to play for Yorkshire he was

' taking ' the finest fast bowling in the country: Allan Hill, the
Lascelles Hall champion; the handsome, bearded George
Freeman, whom Richard Daft and W. G. Grace both thought
the finest fast bowler they had ever played against, and Tom
Emmett, who was more erratic than either, and therefore more
difficult to take, but would frequently put down his unplayable
' sostenutor '. ("What else would you call it?" demanded
Tom.) And as soon as Pinder saw this ball he knew the batsman was done for. There is a record of W. G. Grace having
played the finest innings of his life against the Yorkshire bowling
of Freeman and Emmett at Lord's in 1870, when the balls went
' flying about his ribs, shoulders and head '. But if W. G.
was being battered in this manner, what was happening to poor
George Pinder behind the stumps?

To Pinder it was a sore point that the great Australian
' prince of wicket-keepers ' should regularly be credited with
the honour of being the first wicket-keeper to function without a
long-stop. " I was the man," said Pinder. The game was a
North v. South match, and A. N. Hornby, who was captain,
asked him if he could keep wicket without a long-stop.

" Well, you know, sir," said Pinder, " every time it passes
me it'll be four."

Hornby seemed willing to take the risk, and when one fly-
away ball, probably from Tom Emmett, did go to the boundary,
he was not alarmed. The experiment was regarded as
successful.

So successful was Pinder in his general work that one day at
the Oval Ephraim Lockwood, who was fielding long-stop, said
to him: " Nay, George, I've been behind thee for twenty-three
overs and had nowt to stop. I'm off where there's summat
to do."

Sometimes George's stumping was so slick that the batsman
could not bring himself to believe it, and once when Tom
Hearne, the old Middlesex man, had been stumped by George
off a leg-shooter, he cried out: " I don't call that stumping; I
call it *shovelling of 'em in*!"

He was once, in the carefree atmosphere of Scarborough,

relieved of the cares and callouses of wicket-keeping, and allowed, as a favour, to bowl lobs. Afterwards a member in the pavilion facetiously rallied him on his sinfulness. " You bowl twisters, Mr. Pinder; twisters are intended to deceive, and all deception is sin."

" Then I reckon," returned George ruefully, " every time he hits me to t'boundary it washes my sins away."

You will not find Pinder's name in any of the teams that toured Australia in his time, but he went to America in 1879 with Richard Daft's eleven, and with his cronies, Ulyett and Lockwood, carried a breath of old Yorkshire's moors and mills to and across the New World. The records of these American tours give a good account of the cricket played, but they seldom tell us much about the impression made by the new, hustling, bustling industrial nation then hurtling into being upon those possibly simple-minded characters from the West Riding. The world knows what Ephraim (dear Old Mary Ann) thought of Niagara, but nobody has ever been told what, in their deep, dry, humorous way, those characters thought of the American scene as a whole. Now nobody will ever know.

George Pinder was no more successful than Ted Pooley in making a good thing out of cricket. The financial side of the old professional cricketer's life is shown in a letter written by him to ' Old Ebor '. George was replying with dignity to the rather loudly asserted opinions of some correspondents that professional cricketers were wild fellows, spending their money in wanton extravagance, and generally raising hell. It is a solemn thought that what George, who gave up playing county cricket in 1881, envied most of all was the luxury-ridden players of seventeen years later, who, in addition to their modest summer wages, received £2 a week for ' winter keep '.

> " . . . At the time when I was playing we had not so many matches, and we only got £5 wherever we went. The largest number I played in in one season was twenty-four. That would be £120. Out of that I had to pay my hotel bills, my railway travelling, and maintain my home, wife and four children. We started in May and gave up in September—that is five months—and then we had seven months to get over. So you see we had not a deal to throw away or spend."

There is genuine pathos in this:

"... Gentlemen that used to treat me when I was playing pass me by now. They remark: 'That used to be the best wicket-keeper in England; poor d——l, he has spent all his money and got nothing now.' It is not exactly being poor, but the remarks they make."

There spoke the dignity of a decent man. Everybody should be glad that the players of 1954 enjoy vastly improved conditions; I think few of them, particularly the younger ones, realize exactly how vastly those conditions have improved.

After the rich age of Pooley, Pilling and Pinder, we are approaching the stage at which so many historians start: the age of the Hon. Alfred Lyttelton in England and of J. M. Blackham in Australia. Here were two wicket-keepers supreme in their respective talents; one polished and elegant, the other burning with a fierce efficiency. In the first Test match (1880) ever played on English soil Lyttelton and Blackham gave what was reckoned to be the finest exhibition of wicket-keeping the game had ever seen. Following Lyttelton there were other great amateurs: A. E. Newton of Somerset, who lived to a ripe age and Gregor McGregor, perhaps the finest of all amateur wicket-keepers. In the Lord's Test of 1890 McGregor on one side and Blackham on the other did not let a single bye go past them in the whole of the four innings. Blackham and Lyttelton, Blackham and McGregor; with either pair the quality was superlative.

3

When history hurries along to 'my' time, that is, the first decade of the twentieth century the roll of county wicket-keepers is a muster of masters. Apart from old David Hunter, who had taken over from his elder brother, Joe Hunter, the first wicket-keepers I knew by repute were Lilley (whose nephew I falsely represented myself to be) and Strudwick, who were the stumpers of P. F. Warner's Ashes-winning side of 1903–04. Lilley took over England's gloves from Storer of Derbyshire, who, like his successor, was a powerful and punishing bat, and held them until his retirement in 1911. Strudwick, a keen,

alert and essentially likeable character, was England's reserve to
Lilley in 1903–04, when he was only twenty-three, and went
on two tours after the 1914–18 war. England did not do well
in either of these tours, but whoever played feebly on these
occasions, it was not Strudwick. He came back to the England
side in the triumph of 1926, and when his career ended he had
topped all the wicket-keepers' records for the highest number of
dismissals with a figure of just under 1,500. Since his retirement he has acted as scorer to the Surrey club, and in the
photograph showing the county champions of 1952, the
youngest—and sprightliest-looking member of the group was
Herbert Strudwick. Furthermore, if it be rather pompous to
call Strudwick an elder statesman, it is certain that no county
club ever had a kindlier, wiser ' uncle '.

Every county of ' my ' time had a fine wicket-keeper: for
Kent, Huish, that slightly unpronounceable collaborator in
deception with Colin Blythe; for Gloucester, Jack Board, who
seemed to get banged about far more than the average stumper;
and for Somerset one of the rare amateurs, H. Martyn, who
was almost as brilliant as Gregor McGregor; and besides these
were Harry Butt of Sussex, Stone of Hants and Gaukroger of
Worcestershire, whose odd name was a godsend for contemporary (and rather simple-minded) humorists. All of these
were good men, strong of heart and sore of hand. Most of
them, indeed almost all of them, as I remember, except
Strudwick, who then, compared with the others, seemed a slip
of a lad, wore immense cavalry moustaches which drooped,
nay, cascaded, over their mouths like a plush fringe. David
Hunter's was a large, rich hanging; so was Lilley's; so was
Harry Butt's. The thing became practically a palisade. The
cavalry moustache was the normal decoration (or disfigure-
ment) of the period; perhaps all my wicket-keepers were just a
little more in the fashion than anybody else.

Anybody who has watched cricket for fifty years may well
feel that things in general have not advanced as far as might be
hoped. We do not seem to have the great fast bowlers, though
we have hopes of Moss and Statham and high hopes of True-

man; we have not the great slow bowlers, though we think more than well of Lock. It was said not long ago, and not by Mother Shipton either, but by a critic of superior foresight, that Surrey would never be champions until that county had produced a really first-class slow bowler. Here he is, but where are the others? We certainly have not the great all-rounders, and I say that without disrespect to Trevor Bailey, who is undoubtedly the best we have and did wonders of late. In many ways it seems we are in a ' down ' period, although it is almost certain that we are facing upwards in a courageous struggle to lift ourselves out of it. Yet though certain standards may appear to have declined (if only temporarily), I do not think that wicket-keeping has declined at all. No reasonable person can say that it is any worse than it was half a century ago; I will go further and claim that the general standard is better.

There is an odd parallel here with association football. Always excepting Stanley Matthews and Tom Finney, there is a dearth of quick-thinking, quick-moving forwards, and also of that all-rounder, the attacking half-back, but there is no shortage of excellent goalkeepers. Similarly there are plenty of excellent wicket-keepers. If Godfrey Evans is head and shoulders above all the others, the level on which he looks down is an extraordinarily high one. It does not matter where you go, you will find that, when a team is successful, a good wicket-keeper is playing a big part in that success; when a team is not successful it is not the wicket-keeper who has let the side down. There are good wicket-keepers everywhere, and many of them are comparatively young ones: among these we may count McIntyre, who has toured Australia as a reserve wicket-keeper and bats most attractively, and Spooner, who visited the West Indies earlier in 1954 and is a solid left-handed bat. Besides these, there are Stevenson of Somerset, Dawkes of Derbyshire and Prouton of Hampshire. All are keen, alert and efficient. Another who has been markedly successful is Paul Gibb, who played for Cambridge and for Yorkshire and England as an amateur and now turns out for Essex as a professional. This

was a courageous thing to do, and his success is fully justified.
Gibb is the third wicket-keeper whom Yorkshire, in their
plenty, have allowed to pass to alien shires. The others are
Fiddling, late of Northants, and Firth, now of Leicestershire.
Now that the mercurial Vic Brennan has retired, Yorkshire may
be sorry that they let these fine lads go.   Among the youngsters
I particularly like Parr of Lancashire and Murray of Middlesex
II, both of whom can also bat with commendable stubbornness.
The latter has played only a few times for the first team, but I
believe he will play many more.

The reigning monarch, of course, is Evans. Broadly, there
are two kinds of wicket-keeper: the penny plain and the
tuppence coloured. Evans is fourpence, Technicolored. It is
customary for the austere to look down their longish noses at the
flying leaps of spectacular wicket-keepers. (Dashed un-
British; like a lot of Continental goalkeepers. . . .) But such
strictures do not apply to Evans. He does not turn easy
catches into seeming impossible ones, which is the mark of the
meretricious. His nearly impossible catches he takes without
disturbance, reserving his lateral tiger-springs for the quite
impossible. His highest quality is a little untranslatable.
The French, who order these things better, have a word for it:
panache or *élan*. It is the bloom on the peach, the glitter of the
genuine diamond, the extra brilliance of the perfectly tuned
instrument in the hands of a master. A good deal of nonsense is
talked, and not only by psychologists, about the expression of
personality. For once the phrase is legitimate. Here is the
genuine thing, the expression in cricket of a gay, exuberant
personality. Here is someone who enjoys every moment of
wicket-keeping, even between the overs, and conveys that
enjoyment in a wave that ripples over the boundary's edge and
gives warm pleasure to every soul around it. He seems to have
taken literally the lyrical injunction to ' spread a little happiness ' and to be intent on delivering the order wholesale.
Apart from last winter's West Indian tour, he has appeared
with the utmost credit in forty-nine Tests. No other wicket-
keeper has a more impressive record, except Oldfield, who

played in fifty-four, and Evans is still what actuaries call a good life.

The wicket-keeper is the central figure in the field. He can be the game's hardest worker and, if he is a man with the flash and sparkle of Godfrey Evans, he can at the same time be its greatest entertainer.

CHAPTER VII

ROSES WHITE AND ROSES RED

I

THERE is no better occupation on earth than playing cricket. The next best, if you are too old or too young to play, is watching cricket. You can divide watchable matches into three categories: matches of the past, possibly of the distant past, that you would like to have seen; matches that you have actually seen and possibly gone crazy at; and matches of an ideal character that you hope you may one day see and enjoy. You might, for instance, wish you had seen the palpitating Ashes match of 1882 or Jessop's fabulous match of 1902 or, indeed, any of the three victories so haltingly described in the first chapter of this volume; in the second instance, you carry at least one game in your repertory, which in your flowing cups is freshly remembered; it quickens your pulse and empties the club-lounge at the same time. It is equally certain that there is in your delighted imagination some match with a very desirable result that you would like to see played out: it might be a game in which your own county defeated its deadly local rival, or better still, the Australians. The match which in 1952 I most wanted to see was England's victory at the Oval in 1953, but since that victory has actually happened I sigh for more worlds for Hutton to conquer. The match I now want to see is the one in Sydney in which England make certain that the Ashes are retained for at least one more period.

Of the matches I did not see there were many; of those I could not possibly have seen there were many more. 'Setting aside' Test matches and the most exciting of the Gentlemen v. Players games (as in 1894, when F. S. Jackson and Sammy Woods bowled unchanged through both innings), I should like to have seen some of the earlier encounters—skirmishes or pitched battles—in the unending Wars of the Roses. Of all regional rivalries this is the sharpest-edged. It is a different temper and deeper antagonism than is normally found elsewhere, though I have heard that a State match between New South Wales and Victoria can provide something quite pretty in the way of essential hostility.

War broke out, I understand, in 1849. The county championship proper was not to begin for another twenty-four years, but friendly matches, if that adjective is correct, took place at irregular intervals. Two games were played in 1849 and again in 1851. In 1867 Yorkshire played Lancashire three times and won all three games. This was the beginning of the period when those three tremendous bowlers, George Freeman, Allan Hill and Tom Emmett, were beginning to wage their onslaught and make their mark—sometimes literally—on the batsmen of England. The list of people who thought George Freeman the best fast bowler they had ever played against was long and impressive, starting with W. G. Grace and working downwards. I have sometimes thought that when Alec Bedser retires (and may it be a long time hence) people will say, as for a long period they said after Freeman's retirement: " There is *nobody* now. . . ." This was not, and will not, be true, but it is a measure of Freeman's (and Bedser's) greatness that people felt (and will feel) it to be true at the time.

It was in 1873 that the county championship took real shape, and what seems an astonishing thing to me is that it took Yorkshire exactly twenty years to win it. Over that period they had the best bowlers in the country, and some of the best all-rounders. The English team in the first of all Test matches, played at Melbourne in 1877, contained five Yorkshiremen. During this time when Yorkshire were *not* winning the championship, Freeman, Allan Hill and Tom Emmett were the best fast bowlers, George Ulyett was the best all-rounder, and Peate, whose career was lamentably short, was the best slow bowler the England selectors could find anywhere. In spite of this galaxy of talent, the county team was oddly erratic, beginning the season badly but ending it with brilliance or starting off in winning vein and falling to ultimate disaster. It seems incredible that a side which contained an Ulyett or an Emmett should be accused of slackness in the field, but slackness there was somewhere. During one period in the 'eighties Yorkshire fielding grew so lackadaisical that ill-natured critics said they were too polite to run a man out. Full as the side was of talented individual performers, it was not yet welded into a great team. There were some grand sailors, but they were not a crack crew.

In the Yorkshire *v.* Lancashire match of 1875 that mighty opening pair, Hornby and Barlow, put up a first-wicket stand of just under 150, a big score for those days. The run-stealers flickered to and fro to some purpose that day, and Lancashire won by ten wickets. Incidentally, Hornby's passion for stealing runs was frequently disastrous . . . to his partners. Indeed, one of Lancashire's opponents—it ought to have been Tom Emmett—was once heard to observe: " What a pity Mr. Hornby's gone! Now we shall have to bowl 'em out! "

In 1884 Ulyett did the hat-trick, and in 1887 Yorkshire ran up the score of 590, which remained a record until it was beaten by a score of 887 in 1896. This is still a county record. These were fine matches, but the one I would choose for the first of my three wishes would be the game played at Old Trafford on August Bank Holiday 1893. This was the year when York-shire, after twenty years of struggle, won their first champion-ship, but they did not win this match. The result was in doubt till the very last ball.

2

It happened before I was born, but not very long. My step-Uncle Walter saw it, and the excitement of that game remained with him, glowing warmly, for the rest of his life. You might question the basic wisdom of one who, living in a trim and tranquil inland ' watering-place ', was so misguided as to spend a Bank Holiday in Manchester, but off Uncle Walter went to catch a ' trip ' train early in the morning. The weather, as you might suppose, was threatening, a state of affairs not unknown at Old Trafford. Uncle Walter was a fair-minded man, except when roused to blind passion by the sight of Yorkshire in jeopardy. His patriotism worked through what would nowadays be called a series of regional pacts. He would always support the north against the south; he had, even, a deep respect for Lancashire, except during the rigours of a Yorkshire and Lancashire game. Asked what was his chief impression of this particular match, he would reply: " Funny umpiring."

At Old Trafford that day there was a record crowd of 25,000, not merely to make a show for Uncle Walter, but because the promise of drama was in the air. It must have been one of the fiercest battles ever fought, even between these ancient enemies. Although both sides batted twice, the total score amounted to little more than 200. The top individual score for Lancashire was 21, Yorkshire's leading scorer was J. T. Brown with 17. Lancashire had that formidable opening pair, A. C. MacLaren and Albert Ward; they were not quite so renowned as their predecessors, Hornby and Barlow (then not so long ago), nor was Ward so magical a companion as R. H. Spooner was later to be. Nevertheless MacLaren and Ward formed as capable a pair of opening batsmen as you would then see in any county. At No. 3 came Frank Sugg, a powerful hitter with a fine eye, and after him there was poor Johnny Briggs, then probably the most valuable all-rounder in the country, a punishing bat, a cunningly deceptive slow bowler, a remarkable fielder who could take catches at mid-on or mid-off (or practically anywhere else) off his own bowling. They also had Baker, a conscientious and reliable batsman, and Arthur Mold, the successor of the fiery Crossland and the most intimidating fast bowler of the period. In time he was no-balled for throwing and virtually driven out of cricket, but he had still many wickets to hurl down and many stumps to smash before that misfortune happened to him.

Lancashire won the toss but started badly, and Uncle Walter could hardly believe his eyes when the wickets began to fall. He said that it was half like a nightmare and half like a game of ninepins. MacLaren was taken by George Hirst at mid-off from a drive that with luck would have gone for four; Sugg was picked off in the slips by the first of Tunnicliffe's six catches in the match, and Briggs was out leg-before to Hirst. At this moment of crisis there was a stand of sorts between the patient Ward and S. M. Crosfield, Lancashire's acting captain, but the latter was run out, amid the execrations of the populace, and after that nobody except Baker, a steady bat who afterwards became coach at Harrow School, put up any resistance whatever. The innings closed at 64, finished off by Peel and Ernest Smith, the Yorkshire schoolmaster, who was never seen before August, but could be relied on to turn out for his county directly the summer holidays had begun.

The crowd watched Lancashire's miserable showing with ill-concealed disgust. When the first Yorkshire wicket fell they were slightly bemused; when the second man was out (and it was F. S. Jackson) they were incredulous but delighted; when the third went his way—the score was now *seven*—they were crowing with a kind of delirious bliss. Brown and Tunnicliffe steadied the boat: it is instructive to note that these two were not Yorkshire's Nos. 1 and 2, as they were to become and remain for several years. As a boy, I thought they had been there since time began, but I was wrong. In this match they batted Nos. 4 and 5 and, as it turned out, were responsible for Yorkshire's best stand, not merely of the innings but of the match. Briggs—a regular spring-heeled jack of a man, Uncle Walter called him—was bowling with a kind of jiggly, bouncing deceptiveness, while at the other end Mold literally hurled them down. In Uncle Walter's day, and indeed in ' mine ', it was not thought absurd to open the attack with a very fast bowler at one end and a slow one at the other. The effect upon the batsmen of the contrast was regarded as an attacking weapon in itself. The older bowlers and captains would never, I think, have turned the new ball into a sacred cow and they would have thought present-day seam-worship unseemly. I have seen Hirst and Rhodes open the bowling just as Mold and Briggs, and indeed Hirst himself and Peel did, in this match.

Perhaps my subconscious has led me into this digression in an attempt to divert attention from Yorkshire's frightful collapse.

After Brown and Tunnicliffe, the deluge. Briggs had begun it
and Mold completed it. Only Bobby Peel, who made twelve,
fought with any appearance of confidence, and the rest tumbled
like skittles. I imagine that the appearance of Mold whirling
up to the crease made a tail-end batsman feel exactly like a
skittle. Yorkshire were all out for 58. My agonized relative,
as he sat on his hard wooden seat, surrounded by what seemed
to him the entire population of Manchester, intoxicated with
triumph, is deserving of sympathy even at sixty years' distance.
As the solitary representative of the ranks of Tuscany, he could
well forbear to cheer. MacLaren and Ward made seven without loss before half-past six, and Uncle Walter went home to his
hotel. I doubt if he could have stood any more that evening.

It rained during the night—he heard it beating on his window
—and when he got back to Old Trafford in the morning the
pitch was steaming under a hot sun. The ground was once
more packed, as though nobody had been home. From the
first moment a devil of excitement, a kind of infectious madness,
began to rise like mercury in an overheated thermometer.
It rolled and swelled all round the 25,000 spectators. It invaded the playing arena, rattled the umpires and caused world-
famous batsmen to do things they would not have done had
they been calm and in their right mind. MacLaren and
Ward started off as if they meant to consolidate their small lead
of the previous evening and pile up a good score. They had
got as far as 22, almost as good a stand as any other in the
match, when MacLaren was caught by Hunter behind the
wicket. At least that is what Peel and Hunter appealed for.
MacLaren stood for a moment, angrily incredulous. My Uncle
Walter said that spectators near him told him that spectators
nearer the square-leg boundary heard MacLaren ejaculate:
" Never within an ensanguined mile of it ! " I do not believe
this, but a legend was begun that day and has persisted for
sixty years. Sugg went next, caught by Tunnicliffe, who,
Uncle Walter said, seemed to have as many arms as a hat-rack,
and Briggs, after a dancing hit or two, went the same way
home. The long arm of the law was a novice compared with

Tunnicliffe's. How curiously the pattern of one innings must
have followed that of the other. Just as Briggs had been unplayable, so was Bobby Peel. They were slow left-hand bowlers
of England quality, and few of the batsmen on either side could
do anything with them. All the time they were groping rather
than coping. Peel took six wickets in this innings, Ted Wainwright helping him to finish it off. All of Peel's six victims
were caught behind the wicket, four by Tunnicliffe and two by
Hunter. Besides roaring disapproval at the umpire who gave
MacLaren out, the crowd was in a mood to shout loudly at
anything. Almost everything that happened was outside
normal belief. The continuous dismissal for under double
figures of batsmen who ordinarily made 50 or 100 strained
credulity. Three innings had been completed and only 172 had
been scored altogether. Uncle Walter expected to wake up at
any moment.

But the firm fact was that Yorkshire were left only 57 to
get to win and, if this had not been a ' crazy ' game, it would
have been child's play. F. S. Jackson, who played for England
while still an undergraduate, went in with Arthur Sellars, the
forceful sire of a forceful son, playing steadily and with confidence. Twenty went up, a third of the deficit. Johnny
Briggs was heard to murmur that it was all over bar the
shouting. Then another of the things happened that come
under the heading of ' funny umpiring '. With the score at 24,
Briggs bowled a ball that hit Jackson on the pad and went away
to leg. The batsmen started to run. Suddenly Jackson saw
the umpire's hand raised, and thought that, however daft the
decision, he had been given out. For a moment he stood still,
well out of his ground. The whole of Old Trafford was in
pandemonium. The bowler's umpire explained, with a wealth
of pantomime, that he had only been signalling a leg-bye.
In the general madness, the ball was returned to A. T. Kemble,
the stumper, who, seeing the bewildered Jackson out of his
ground, promptly knocked off the bails, shouting: " How's
that? "

" What for? " demanded the square-leg umpire.

" Stumped."

" Not out."

" Then, run out," persisted Mr. Kemble, presumably think-ing he would try anything once.

" Out," returned the umpire, raising his right hand as solemnly and unmistakably as though taking an oath.

And out Jackson went. So did Brown. So did Tunnicliffe. So did Wainwright. But the larger lunacy was not yet exor-cised. Ernest Smith hit a skimming drive, almost on the carpet, a certain four ' all the way '. Crosfield made a wild goalkeeper's dive and was seen—by those who saw anything—to throw the ball up in the air. Almost everybody was shouting. The umpire hesitated. Smith could not believe that a catch had been made. When the umpire's finger went up, Smith still could not believe it. It was genuine incredulity and not defiance of the rules. As Uncle Walter said : " He practically had to have a letter of explanation before he'd go, and I don't blame him."

Yorkshire's batting then descended into the abyss. The baying of the crowd had scarcely time to die down between the batsmen's entry and departure. Of all the four ' processions ' this was the most abject. From the prospect of an easy victory (24 for 0) Yorkshire found themselves staggering on the edge of defeat (46 for 7). The one genuinely imperturbable person was Happy Jack Ulyett, the man who eleven years before had gone in first for England with W. G., and wondered at the time why everybody was so nervous of Spofforth. It must have been odd to see this hero of many Tests coming in to bat at No. 9, but he was in his last season and approaching the elder statesman class. The three wickets still outstanding were those of Moor-house, Hirst and Hunter, and so long as the first two of these were ' alive ' Ulyett knew that it was his business to play steadily and even get 'em in singles. But the back of his strategy was rudely broken. Moorhouse, who should have stood his ground at all costs, leaped out to a temptingly innocent ball from Briggs and was stumped. Hirst came next, a fine, strong lad of twenty-three. George Hirst at No. 10 would seem as irrational to a later age as George Ulyett at No. 9 would have appeared to an earlier one. Yorkshire played him first as a straight fast bowler—straight in every sense of the word—but his batting began to improve almost from the start, and in the previous match with Gloucestershire he had scored an undefeated 35 out of a meagre Yorkshire total. ("I had no idea," said W. G. Grace with rueful appreciation, "that the beggar could bat so well too.") But to-day was not George's day. He made one of his tremendous pulls and saw it well caught by Baker. The situation, once critical, was now desperate. It was here that Ulyett was faced with the problem well known to leaders of desperate enterprises. In came David Hunter, who, though near to being an England wicket-keeper, was far from being an England batsman. He scored a shaky single and then Ulyett was in charge. Six runs were wanted and there was one way of scoring six that appealed to Happy Jack. There have always been those who said that Ulyett lashed out because he could not stand the strain of the excitement, but Uncle Walter would not accept this explanation at any price. "He knew what he was about," said he. "He had the right idea: he knew he couldn't trust David and that hitting one walloping sixer was the only way to do it. And he nearly did it, and all."

Down came Johnny Briggs's innocent ball—a ball that would have tempted St. Anthony—and Ulyett hit it fair and square. Up it soared, a sixer if ever there was one. Uncle Walter's hat and the ball were in the air at the same moment. Down came the ball at last. Surely, surely it was going straight over the boundary. But no. At the boundary, leaning as though by accident on the rails, was Albert Ward, his great frame bent backwards and his hands like a carpet-bag. A shorter man could never have got anywhere near it, but into that carpet-bag went the ball and the match was over. Uncle Walter never saw his hat again, but there were hundreds of Lancashire hats in the air, and as they came down Uncle Walter took a flying drop-kick at one of them. It seemed the simplest way of relieving his feelings. Happy Jack himself had no doubt that what he had done was the right thing, and years afterwards he declared that he would have made the same attempt to hit the same six.

"I thought it was better," he said, "to make the runs if I could while I was facing Johnny Briggs. So I went for the boundary, but Albert was on the edge of it and we lost. . . . It shows how little you can be certain of in cricket."

And that, according to an admittedly biased account, is what happened in the ' mad ' match of 1893; a match in which one future England captain swore audibly at the umpire, and another allowed himself to be run out through not standing his ground during a hubbub; a distinguished schoolmaster had to be specifically ordered by the umpire to leave the crease and, finally, my Uncle Walter, one of the gentlest souls who ever breathed, kicked a hole in the top hat of a Manchester gentleman who had never done him any harm. It just shows you. . . .

3

I am not sure which was the most enthralling Roses match I ever saw myself. To the initiated, every Lancashire · v. Yorkshire match is enthralling, because of its rigour, its essential combativeness, its sense of being a battle in which no quarter is given or solicited. Strangers who are not conversant with local history and character have been known to consider these yearly encounters dull. They criticize the tactics but do not understand the grand strategy of the struggle. They do not understand the burning intensity of the individual endeavour. They do not understand. . . .

Yorkshire v. Lancashire matches, like any other hundred years' war, fall naturally into different phases. A fact which cannot be insisted on too strongly is that the grim no-fours-before-lunch aspect of the struggle was a passing phenomenon of a particular time between the two world wars. It was characteristic of a period, not of a people. It did not happen before the first war and it has not happened to any great extent since the second one. In the earliest matches that I saw there was dash and brilliance, and any number of fours before lunch.

You could not conceive drabness as coming from teams that included MacLaren, Spooner and Tyldesley on one side and Jackson, Denton and Hirst on the other. The 1903 match at Bradford was a long battle of swaying fortunes. Each side collapsed in turn, as it had collapsed at Manchester ten years before—Lancashire before Rhodes (twice) and Yorkshire before the great Sydney Barnes. (This was during the comparatively short period that Barnes consented to play for Lancashire.) A stand for the ninth wicket by A. Eccles and that sturdy all-rounder, Willis Cuttell, saved Lancashire's first innings from virtual extinction while Yorkshire, after a good start, collapsed without apparent reason and finished up only five runs ahead. In Lancashire's second innings Rhodes so dominated the batsmen that five wickets fell for just over 50, and at close of play on Bank Holiday Tuesday the score was 88 for seven. Next morning, however, a young footballer named Jack Sharp—he made a century for England at the Oval six years later after being picked as a fast bowler—proceeded to knock Rhodes to glory, reducing his analysis to a mere eight for 61. Yorkshire's leading batsmen faltered, and over 50 runs were still wanted when, with five wickets down, Rhodes joined Hirst. The way those two hit off the runs was thrilling in the extreme. From start to finish there was not a hit made or a ball bowled or fielded without firm and vivid purpose.

The game I remember best was the one that took place at Sheffield on August Bank Holiday in 1905. Uncle Walter and I were involved in some family duties on the Monday and we did not travel to Sheffield till the Tuesday morning. I remember rising incredibly early and sleeping most of the way in the train. We had missed the previous day's play, but we knew from 'Old Ebor' the appalling things that had happened. If I had not been so sleepy I should have shuddered at the very thought. A man called Walter Brearley had battered Yorkshire almost to a pulp. Seven for 35, that was what this fiend in human form had done to us. Yorkshire had been dismissed for a trumpery 76, out of which Jackson had made 30 and Tunnicliffe 17. Neville Cardus once said that as a small boy at

Old Trafford he would pray that one of the Yorkshire bowlers—
the one who was getting the wickets at the time—would drop
down dead. I never went quite so far as that, but on several
occasions I prayed that Providence would do something about
Walter Brearley. When Jackson and Tunnicliffe had gone, the
next highest score was Schofield Haigh's six.

After this holocaust MacLaren and Spooner gave their side
an even more than usually splendid start. Before that shining
pair were separated they had already passed Yorkshire's
miserable total and, although nobody else except Tyldesley did
very much, Lancashire started the next day nearly 100 runs
ahead with two wickets to fall. So there we were, my uncle and
I, with what George Meredith called ' a great ocean of a day
before us '.

It was my first visit to Bramall Lane, and I was awed partly
by the size of the crowd and partly by the murk that, even on
that comparatively fair day, hung about the ground like the
pillar of cloud that guided the Israelites in the wilderness.
The two Lancashire wickets soon fell and Brearley, the last
man, seemed to gallop to the wicket, where he was clean
bowled by Jackson, and back again, as though he hardly intended to stop. He was obviously anxious to get to work on
the more serious business of life. While Yorkshire were in
jeopardy, life was too anxious for enjoyment. I blenched when
Brearley bowled Tunnicliffe and trembled when he sent cart-
wheeling the middle stump of Jimmy Rothery, a fellow-townsman
of ours, to whom we had particularly wished to bring luck.
But our fervent prayers availed naught.

" Jackson'll show them," said Uncle Walter, sucking his pipe
with the grim optimism of a man who might just as well be
hopeful as anything else.

Jackson received a mighty cheer as he strode to the wicket.
He was captain of England that year; a confident and winning
captain, who, whatever he might do for his county, had never
let his country down. But it was not Jackson, great man
though he was, who was the hero of that day.

David Denton was Yorkshire's most dashing bat. There was

a gaiety in his attack. That year he was playing with the ease and confidence of a master. He was well in line for the position of England's No. 3—he had played for England once that season—and only one thing kept him from regular tenure of that post of honour: the genius of Tyldesley. Everything Denton did, Tyldesley did better; not immensely better, but sufficiently better to keep Denton out of the England side, except on that one occasion when he got in owing to an injury to Fry. Uncle Walter was a fanatical Yorkshireman, but this never finally blinded him to the facts of life. He knew that Denton was not quite the England man that Tyldesley was. This was quite apart from the fact that Tyldesley was one of the most popular cricketers wherever he went, both for the brilliance of his play and the integrity of his character. Uncle Walter knew. . . . But this knowledge did not spoil his appreciation of Denton's splendour that day, for that was Denton's day.

Jackson was an England man and, especially on that season's showing, by far the best all-rounder in England, but for once Denton eclipsed him. If there was a stroke on the board that he did not play, I still do not know what it was. He cut Brearley to the boundary time after time in a way that made you think of Ranji, and when, as it seemed to us, the bowler bowled at his head, he hooked him away to square-leg with a kind of gay ferocity, despatching bumpers where bumpers ought to be despatched. He was more dazzling on the off than the on, flinging off square-cuts and cover drives in a careless glittering star-shower. We saw more than one streaky one go flying through the slips, but we felt that so dashing a performer was entitled to all the luck that came his way.

"They can't set a field to him," chuckled Uncle Walter. "They can't do it."

And now Jackson was beginning to score too. His shots had not the positive dazzle and sheen upon them that Denton's had, but they sped to the boundary as if propelled by a sort of elemental force. After this remarkable stand both batsmen departed practically together. Denton just missed his century by the four he did not get when MacLaren caught him in the slips off a ferocious slash. Jackson missed his fifty, Hirst was out for half a dozen, and just as the first cracks of another collapse were about to open up, Rhodes stepped in. He was tall and of a ruddy countenance and he scored almost as quickly as Denton, with firm, handsome strokes mostly on the leg. Nobody else made many, but Rhodes hit hard and nursed his weaker brethren. Uncle Walter became involved in a friendly argument with his neighbour on the right, who observed:

" One of t'best bats in England, Wilfred."

" I'd hardly say that," returned Uncle Walter judicially. " He's doing grandly to-day, but we need his *bowling* more than his batting. . . ."

" You'll see," persisted our neighbour.

Well, another five years proved that the Sheffielder was right. Another twenty-one years proved that Uncle Walter was right. Those who live longest, as Uncle Walter said, see most.

Rhodes may have played some more impressive innings in his later, greater batting days, but never a happier or more valuable one. As long as he was at the crease Yorkshire had a fighting chance, but when he was out all seemed to be over. Lancashire were set only 185 to win, and before half-past six they had knocked off 50 of these. Haigh had bowled Spooner with one of his tremendous break-backs, while Jackson had dismissed the lordly MacLaren, an act of *lèse-majesté* in itself, but Tyldesley was still in, and we left the ground with the feeling that Lancashire would easily knock off the runs.

We stayed the night with an aunt of my step-uncle's, a person who now sounds almost like a character out of a Dubonnet advertisement. She was an old lady who wore a white lace cap and gave us ham and lettuce for ' tea ' at eight o'clock. She also sent us off the following morning with large packages of food. You can imagine we were at the ground early; indeed, I was hungrily munching one of my luncheon sandwiches when play began. Tyldesley was partnered by L. O. S. Poidevin, an Australian doctor who had settled in Manchester. His was one of the names which, as a boy, used to roll round my tongue with murderous mispronunciation and deep romantic satisfaction: L. O. S. Poidevin, L. C. H. Palairet, R. N. R. Blaker, B. J. T. Bosanquet. Their names were for me like a muster-roll of the knights of Charlemagne. But I did not feel romantic about Poidevin that day. He treated the Yorkshire bowling severely. While Tyldesley hit beautifully, Poidevin hit hard, and Yorkshire seemed to have no chance while those two were together. As happened so often, it was Haigh who broke the partnership, hitting Tyldesley's stumps with a rattle that might have been caused by a very fast bowler. Whenever I see a modern bowler bowling ' defensively ' off the wicket all afternoon I think of Schofield Haigh, who hit the stumps more than any bowler of his time. It was only the third wicket that fell when Haigh broke through Lancashire's defences, but it was the beginning of the end. The pillar of cloud closed in over the ground. It grew slowly darker as in the famous battle between Tweedledum and Tweedledee. Rhodes at the other end tempted Poidevin out of his ground and then caught and bowled Garnett, who could not resist having a go. After that only Cook managed to score a few; Rhodes made another clever catch off his own bowling; there was a quick run out through a lightning return by Hubert Myers; and then Brearley, scurrying to the wicket, hit a ball high in the air to long-on and Ernest Smith came in and judged it nicely. The great game was over, and Yorkshire had won, against all expectation, by 44 runs. I was the luckiest boy in the world. I had witnessed a battle of giants; I had seen great men: MacLaren, Spooner, Tyldesley and Brearley; and I had seen these great ones excitingly conquered by my own heroes: Hirst, Rhodes and Haigh; Denton and Jackson.

" What do you think of it, lad? "

I clasped his hand tightly, but I could not speak. I have never been quite so happy since. Bliss was it in that dawn to be alive.

4

The Yorkshire v. Lancashire match that I should like to see would be between composite teams of all periods, but I hesitate to pick the sides.   This is a thing that the best of friends cannot agree on.   Once bitten, twice shy.   The last time I picked a series of all-time teams I received, as they say, shoals of letters, all of them written under stress of emotion and most of them abusive.   The kindest word my correspondents used was Barabbas, and that was only because it alliterated so neatly with all the other names they called me.   Each generation thinks the heroes of its boyhood the best, and only the truly great ones from another period, before or since, have a chance of breaking through.   For example, I would pick no all-time Yorkshire (or indeed England, or World) eleven without Hirst, Rhodes and Jackson.   But I would drop the wonderful Brown and Tunnicliffe of my time in order to bring in Hutton from the present and Sutcliffe from the middle period.   As between Denton and Percy Holmes I would not quarrel.   Both were superlatively attractive attacking batsmen; both were more or less permanently kept out of the England side, one by Tyldesley, the other by Hobbs.   I would settle for either, so long as I could have Maurice Leyland at No. 4.   On the other hand, it would be a heartbreaking choice between Haigh and George Macaulay, both superb bowlers of their kind.   I think Haigh might have it by a fraction, if only because of the way he kept on hitting the stumps.   I will allow anybody to pick the wicket-keeper, for Yorkshire have never had a bad wicket-keeper from Pinder to the present day.   There is not one who has not, or could not have, played for England.   If I must declare a name, let it be Arthur Wood.

For me to pick an all-time Lancashire team would be both easier and a greater impertinence; easier, at any rate, because I might be less prejudiced.   But should I?   I should, at any rate, be prejudiced in favour of my own period and start with MacLaren, Spooner and Johnnie Tyldesley.   And I should be right, for MacLaren and Spooner outshone even my Hornby and my Barlow long ago.   No county in any period has had a better trio at the head of its lists.   It is from No. 4 onwards that the trouble would start.   What kind of a choice am I going to make between Washbrook, Paynter and (especially) that splendid batsman, Ernest Tyldesley, the only man besides his brother J. T. to make 30,000 runs for Lancashire? And what of Watson, Makepeace and Hallows, not to mention Ikin and Winston Place? For a wicket-keeper, I am again on fairly safe ground: Duckworth of the iron lungs has it, with Farrimond, who played for England and Lancashire Second, as his reserve. Even then I may have chosen wrong, because I have missed out Pilling, one of the great triumvirate of stumpers, Pooley, Pinder and Pilling. Alas, he died young—he was only thirty-five—but he was reckoned the best in England in his day.

I never saw A. G. Steel, any more than I saw Hornby and Barlow, but the records show him to have been one of the best all-rounders who ever played for Marlborough, Cambridge, the Gentlemen or England. As for bowlers, I should hardly dare to open my mouth, except to say Macdonald would undoubtedly come into an all-time Lancashire and probably an all-time Australian eleven. And if I pick Macdonald as my fast bowler, what becomes of the faithful and forceful Walter Brearley? If he is dropped there will be the devil of a row. There always was. Once when he had been dropped from a Test team he went and stood under the box of the chairman of selectors, beside the clock-tower at Lord's, and began to mutter in a voice audible at least as far as the Nursery: " I always take six wickets and generally the leading batsmen. And I never trust my slips, so I generally clean bowl 'em. . . ."

As for the other bowlers I am dumb. If I cannot have Brearley, I cannot have Statham. And who is going to make a choice from a list that contains Johnny Briggs, Cecil Parkin, the funniest of ' funny ' bowlers, and Dick Tyldesley and Roy Tattersall, for whom I have the greatest admiration, or Harry Dean, that true Lancashire lad, who bowled so finely in Fry's winning Test side in 1912? I can only repeat, I am glad it is not my duty to settle the matter. If it was, I should probably plump for those two elevens of 1905 who brought the highest happiness to me long ago and far away.

CHAPTER VIII

GIVE ME LASCELLES HALL

I

THREE miles out of Huddersfield there is a village on the top of a hill. Its beautiful little cricket ground lies on a broad flat spur of a loftier hill, and, as you stand at the wicket, a wide vista of high fields opens out before you, enchantingly green and hedged like the squares on a chess-board. Its boundary markings are clean and clear, and on the ' top ' side of the field a rubble wall acts as a wind-breaker, for there is plenty of wind on these high levels. The old pavilion, with its pigeon-hole score-box and its board floor spiked by innumerable cricket boots, has itself seen almost a century. More famous matches have been played on this upland than on any other village ground. For beauty and renown even Hambledon's Broad Halfpenny Down cannot surpass the glories of Lascelles Hall.

A hundred and thirty years ago, Lascelles Hall was a hamlet consisting of a gentleman's residence and a handful of grey stone cottages inhabited by hand-loom weavers and their families. These weavers, who worked in their homes, were men of fine physical presence and strong individual character, and there was something in every movement of their daily labour which by its very nature developed a quickness of eye, hand and foot and stood them in splendid stead when they came to their favourite pastime of cricket. What is more, they were sturdily linked in a community of work and play which made them claim to be the happiest, brightest village in England.

Nobody knows when the lads of the village, in their knicker-bockers and clogs, first began to play, using a ball of crewelled yarn and a bit of paling or a weaver's seat-board for a bat, but it is a historical fact that in 1825 a number of lads were caught ' laking ' in a prohibited area near to the Hall itself, a building of grey stone surrounded by a high wall. While most of the others ran away, two of the lads, George Jessop and John Hudson, went up to the Hall to confess their sins. This virtue was happily rewarded, for the Squire's lady persuaded her husband to grant the local lads a playground, and this remained theirs for twenty-one years. After a short break, the privilege was restored, continuing until 1866, when the present ground, in its matchless setting, was brought into being. For their first practice ground, the weavers set up their stumps in a quarry, and later, in the 'fifties, they were given a small field, called the Croft, which had a stone wall along one side. As their wicket was pitched, the wall closed up its onside, and legend tells that because of this, the Lascelles Hall batsmen excelled in beautiful strokes on the off-side. Ephraim Lockwood, the most famous of them, was without peer in his day as a late- and square-cutter. Imagination reels from what Ephraim would have thought of the modern batsman who plays everything on the leg with his pads and leaves everything on the off alone. Even before the turn of the century he was saying in his own dry way: " Now they let 'em go on the off-side. I have seen when I would have given two shillings a dozen for them. I should have got talent money out of it. . . ."

There can never have been greater keenness than existed among the Lascelles Hall weavers. They would practise every moment of their spare time. They called no man master and obeyed no mill-hooter. If they went out for half an hour at dinner-time to practise a late cut or a yorker, they might well stay longer than they intended and if they did, they made up the time on the work by candle-light far into the night. Their rules for practice were strict. Each man received forty balls for batting practice. Any batsman who persisted in staying at the wicket after he had had his quota of forty balls was fined a penny. The ball was rapidly thrown from hand to hand for fielding practice till the next batsman was ready. (The first Australian team I ever saw did this, as part of their normal routine in the field.) If you were in arrears with your subscription by 1st June the Lascelles Hall committee fined you twopence.

C. B. FRY

"*Not merely a supremely talented individual: he is a one-man Ministry of All the Talents...*"

K. S. RANJITSINHJI

"*Possibly one of the three greatest...*"

M. P. DONNELLY

"*Oxford's finest all-round athlete since the great W. G. Owen-Smith.*"

L. N. CONSTANTINE

"*Symbolises the fire, the dash, the bounding vitality of the West Indies.*"

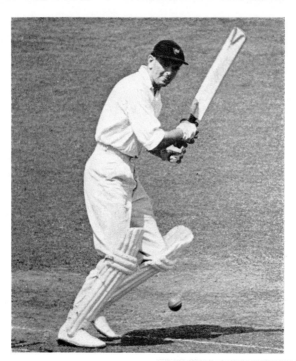

T. W. GRAVENEY

"The idol of every Gloucestershire schoolboy from eight to eighty . . ."

NAWAB OF PATAUDI

" His feat in the University match was more memorable than anything in the history of the series . . ."

The laying of their ground was an admirable corporate effort, though they did not call it that. The club in 1866 had over ninety members. All of them drew lots as to who should do the job of levelling and turf-laying. It is a sad little sidelight on industrial history that this task took place during the aftermath of the American Civil War, when many a hand-loom weaver was idle. The final blow to the hand-loom weaving was the triumphant advent of the power-loom. Once the ground was sown with fine lawn seed and white clover it was tended with care by a succession of local groundsmen, who were paid a shilling a night. The best known of these groundsmen was John Lockwood, Ephraim's cousin—everybody in Lascelles Hall was *somebody's* cousin—of whom it was significantly said that " he could knit turf as if it were fine-drawn ".

Cricket ran in families, and families ran in Lascelles Hall; although hand-loom weaving has been devoured by the machine, the family names remain the same: the Amblers, the Greenwoods, the Thewlises, the Lockwoods, the Redfearns. These families formed the hard core which was the centre of Lascelles Hall cricket. In 1866 a team consisting wholly of Thewlises played a match at Lascelles Hall and won. The umpire, the scorer and the man who took your money at the gate were all Thewlises, too.

It is impossible to exaggerate the keenness of the Lascelles Hall folk when a game was going on; the weavers and their families were all there. There was high feasting, Nyren tells us, on Broad Halfpenny Down when a big match was on. " And then, what stuff they had to drink! " In its more modest way, Lascelles Hall did not do so badly. In 1882 provisions for the Harrow Wanderers and Uppingham matches included:

$\frac{1}{2}$ gallon Scotch whisky, 1 gallon brandy,
$\frac{1}{2}$ gallon rum, 9 boxes ginger beer, 30 lb. beef,
2 hams, 12 dozen pies,

for the first day. There is no record in the club minutes of how they appeased their hunger and thirst on the second day.

It was said that during the solemnity of one of the grand

E

Hambledon matches the multitude formed a complete and dense circle round Broad Halfpenny Down's noble green. But the spectators at Lascelles Hall were no ' fine brown-faced fellows of farmers '. They were the hand-loom weavers; their sons, who were there to learn from the great ones how to get into the first eleven; and their womenfolk, who were as knowledgeable as themselves and who did not hesitate to call out their comments. The young women came to see their heroes and the elderly ones to show their knowledge with all the force and forthrightness of Yorkshire Annie at Lord's to-day. Ladies, by order of the Committee, were admitted at half price.

Nyren has boasted in matchless prose how little Hambledon, pitted against all England, was a proud thought for Hampshire. In 1867 Lascelles Hall, too, was pitted against an all-England eleven of great strength and beat it by six runs. In the 'sixties and 'seventies they had several matches in which they beat strong Yorkshire teams, and in 1874 they defeated a powerful Surrey eleven, captained by the famous Harry Jupp and containing half a dozen of the great players of the day, by an innings. This was perhaps their greatest achievement, in which John Thewlis, Ephraim Lockwood and Luke Greenwood made good scores and Joe Ambler took seven wickets for 63.

The most exciting of their matches was one played in 1870 against a formidable Sheffield eleven which contained such stalwarts as George Pinder and Joe Rowbotham. The game, which was played for £50 a side, arose as the result of a bet made by Ephraim Lockwood with a Sheffield publican whom he met in a cab. (What a man Ephraim must have been to meet in a cab!) The stake was £50, but ever afterwards Luke Greenwood maintained that it could just as well have been £500, if the Sheffielders had wanted.

" The old weavers," said Luke, " used to put down their money on us *like bricks.*" It was one of the hardest battles ever fought even at Bramall Lane. Lascelles Hall, stiffened by sturdy contributions from Andrew Greenwood, David Eastwood and John Thewlis, knocked up 210, after which Pollard,

Allan Hill and Luke Greenwood rattled out their opponents for 106. Sheffield did better when they followed on, but in the end they set Lascelles Hall only 82 to get to win. There was seething excitement when they started on this task, an excitement which tottered into palpitations when four wickets, including the great Ephraim's, fell for six runs. The Lascelles Hall supporters, who had come in every kind of vehicle from wagonettes to farm-carts, were in despair. But David Eastwood and Luke Greenwood, with great coolness and courage, came together in the moment of crisis and weathered the storm. It is said that one old gentleman, who had only come to the ground to protest against the iniquity of betting on the match, flung his hat into the air when the winning hit was made and, as it came down, placed it on his head with great dignity and the side to the front. As a local lyrist put it:

> We scored 210, my friends, against Sheffield's 106,
> I am sure that put the Sheffielders all in a fix;
> But in their second innings they made a better stand,
> Owing to the batting of Stephenson who came out bat in hand.
> Now when we had got Sheffield all out, the Lascelles Hall went in
> To try and win that £100—we wanted 82 to win;
> But when five men were out for 6, the odds were five to four;
> But Luke Greenwood and Dave Eastwood soon rubbed off the score.

2

The heroes of Lascelles Hall were many, and no fewer than twenty-one of them played for their county during the great period of the club, which was roughly between the 'sixties and the 'eighties. Two of them, Andrew Greenwood and Allan Hill, travelled half-way across the world and played alongside Happy Jack Ulyett and Tom Emmett in the first of all Test matches at Melbourne in 1877.

The first to come into prominence was that fine all-rounder, Luke Greenwood, whose name went well with his keen, clean-shaven face and short goatee beard. In the 'sixties many gentlemen ran a private cricket team on their estates, and Luke played four seasons for Lord Lichfield's eleven, during which time he put up some fine performances against George Parr's

All-England side. From there he graduated, by way of North and South matches, to Yorkshire and then to representative games for the Players. His first Gentlemen v. Players match at the Oval was also W. G. Grace's, not to mention Alfred Shaw's, so that, in his own words, he ' came out ' in big matches in very good company. He prided himself on bowling dead straight and claimed that he bowled no more than one wide in his county career, and that was at the Oval after a thunderstorm. Tom Emmett was the chief of sinners in that respect but, to be fair, he took over 1,200 wickets in his county career and Luke took less than 100. When Luke was old and down on his luck he used to walk from his home at Ossett, near Wakefield, to watch a match at Leeds, Bradford or Huddersfield. One Sunday night he set off to watch Yorkshire play Sussex at Sheffield, but when somebody told him that Ranji was not playing he walked back again. Of all the tributes ever paid to the genius of Ranji, that was one of the most sincere.

The second Yorkshire giant from Lascelles Hall was John Thewlis, who came into county cricket late in life. "I was thirty-five," he told ' Old Ebor ' many years later. " I hear they're retiring 'em at that age now."

When he first played for Lascelles Hall in an away match the spectators shouted to him to take his jacket off. He dared not, because of the holes in his shirt, but he made enough runs for them to remember him by. When he was introduced by Luke Greenwood to big cricket he was clean bowled by the first ball he received, and as he passed the bowler on his way to the pavilion he said : " Tha'll none bowl me first ball again, tha can bet." But Thewlis, excellent bat as he was, is chiefly remembered for his famous opening stand at the Oval with his more famous nephew, Ephraim Lockwood. It is an oft-told, but not threadbare, tale. The year was 1868. In the week-end before Yorkshire's match with Surrey at the Oval two of their players were injured in a bus accident and substitutes were needed. For one, Thewlis suggested his young nephew, Ephraim Lockwood. Tom Emmett agreed, and Ephraim was not merely wired for, but put in to bat first. Despite his youth and rawness, he batted like a veteran. At the end of the day he had made 57 and his uncle 51. The next day Ephraim went on to make 91, and the opening stand of uncle and nephew reached 176, which remained a county record for a great many years. There was great speculation as to who, or what, this slip of a lad could be, and as he and his uncle strode back to the pavilion undefeated, Ephraim heard the Surrey supporters wonder aloud. Some thought he was a farmer's boy and some a collier. And one uttered the classic phrase that has come down to us: " Why, he's more fit to eat a penny cake than play cricket." To the picture of Ephraim's triumphant debut is to be added an endearing vignette of Tom Emmett, who had helped his uncle to sponsor him, bringing him out a drink in the heat of the afternoon and saying in his fatherly way: " Think on, tha's on thi merits."

He played for Yorkshire for sixteen years. Sometimes they called him Old Mary Ann and sometimes Big Feet. Indeed, it was said that he could have run faster if he had worn smaller boots. Whatever the size of his feet, however, it did not interfere with the deftness of his cutting. This, like Ranji's famous leg-glance, was no mere deflection, but a hard ' chop ', square with the face of the bat and propelled by a perfectly timed turn of the wrist. He could cut a ball off the middle stump time after time. Few batsmen have ever had the skill and confidence to do this continuously. Ranji, Trumper and Johnnie Tyldesley could have done it, or Macartney and Hammond in a later age. But who else? Ephraim Lockwood's contemporary reputation stands virtually as it did: " There was never a cutter like him." So much was he regarded as the backbone of the team that when he (No. 2) was out, then George Pinder would say to Allan Hill at No. 11 : " Come on, Allan, get thi' pads on; old Mary Ann's out."

Ephraim never went to Australia. He received at least one invitation, but was unable to accept it at the time because he was suffering from acute rheumatism, a complaint which, by any other name, such as ' fibrositis ' or ' slipped disc ', would be just as painful. He did, however, visit America with Richard

Daft's team in 1879, and it was then that he made his classic observation: " If this is Niagara, give me Lascelles Hall." But in this he may have been moved, not so much by disrespect for the world's most famous cataract, as by the attention of the local mosquitoes, which bit his face to such an extent that it ' looked like a pudding '.

There was something essentially good-tempered about Ephraim: something slow, except, of course, in his offside hitting and fielding, something quiet and equable that made it safe for the other fellows to try out their jokes on him Like most of the other Yorkshire professionals of his day, he took his turn at captaining the county side, but it was said of him that he was not a success because ' he lacked firmness owing to his desire to please '. It is plain to see what a nice fellow he was. He was not a bubbling, bouncing spirit like George Ulyett, nor a rip-roaring outsize schoolboy like Tom Emmett, who spent three parts of his time shouting with laughter at the sheer fun of cricket and the other part ' calling himself everything ' for his infrequent mistakes. Once, when he missed a simple return catch from W. G., he threw down his cap and jumped on it. He should not have kicked the ball to the boundary, which only gave W. G. four more runs, and he spent the rest of the day apologizing to him. " I were mad wi` mi-sen. . . . ' That was what Tom always said.   There was also the occasion when he accidentally ran out Luke Greenwood. " If we'd lost the match," he said, " I'd never have shown my face in t'pavilion! " He was ' mad with hissen ' that day, because the square-leg fielder was masked by the square-leg umpire. But Ephraim did not need to be mad with himself. His temperament was placid rather than mercurial. You are not affectionately known as Mary Ann unless you deserve it. He married a niece of the great old cricketer, Fuller Pilch, and because she knew as much about cricket as he did, they lived happily ever after.

He remained modest and self-effacing from the time when he was a ' quiet and unassuming colt ' to the time when he said to his equally famous interviewer: " Nay, I have nowt to say. . . ." There are some cricketers to-day who might do well to have ' nowt to say '.

The best bowler, and the unluckiest player, to come from the Lascelles Hall club was Allan Hill. He was born at Kirkheaton, the village famous for ever as the birthplace of Hirst and Rhodes, but his family moved early to Lascelles Hall, and he grew up there like the rest of the boys, as a weaver, half-mad on cricket. Also like the more famous of the lads, he took his first professional engagement as a ' Saturday man ' at half a crown a time. Afterwards he received five shillings a match, and one of the things he remembered best was his parents' delight when he took home the proceeds of three matches, a whole fifteen shillings. For two years he held a groundsman's job at Stonyhurst, going straight from the hand-loom to the school. After that, while doing another job in Lancashire, he was sent for to play for Yorkshire against Surrey at the Oval, because George Freeman, the county's great fast bowler, had been injured. Never can a fast bowler have had a more startling entry into first-class cricket. Allan Hill opened the bowling with Tom Emmett, and from the first over quite eclipsed the great man. His figures were six for 33, and the rattle of stumps became almost monotonous. When Yorkshire went in they did almost as badly, except for Allan himself, who, though no batsman, made a courageous 28 out of 100! In Surrey's second innings Hill tore through their defences, and again he kept hitting the stumps through perfect length and sheer pace. In all he had taken twelve wickets for 56 runs and every single one of his victims was bowled clean as a whistle.

After that for twelve years he played regularly for Yorkshire, giving of his best, bowling like a magnificent machine, fielding at the cannon's mouth, and occasionally batting like a hero. He never achieved 50; but he got several twenties and thirties at moments of emergency and twice he made 49, once in the second of all Test matches, when he was run out, and once in a vital county game against Middlesex at Bramall Lane. Of this 49 Tom Emmett said: " Nay, Allan, tha'll never get talent-money unless tha bustles t'Committee." His notable bowling feats were difficult to count and his hat-tricks were frequent; one of these took place in the Lord's Gentlemen *v.* Players match of 1874 and included A. N. Hornby among its victims; another took in W. G. himself.

The feat Allan Hill was proudest of was one of neither batting nor bowling. It was one of the annual Roses battles in which Lancashire were set under a hundred to win. 'Monkey' Hornby was in good shape and victory for Lancashire seemed well in sight when Tom Emmett sent down one of the worst balls ever bowled, a long-hop wide on the off. Hornby lashed out at it with all his might; it hit Allan Hill's hands with a smack like hitting a board and stuck. After this staggering catch he went on to bowl at the other end and took five for 3.

His county career ended sadly in an accident. He had had several minor ones, including the time of the Gloucestershire match of 1874, when, if he had not had to stand down, there would have been seven Lascelles Hall men in the Yorkshire team. In 1884 he fell after a violent collision with the wicket-keeper in trying to snatch a single in a match at Birmingham. His collar-bone was fractured, and he was never strong enough to bowl in county cricket again.

3

Fascinating as the Lascelles Hall club's history has been, it is only one village of many. The Huddersfield district is rich in local clubs which have sprung up at various periods during the nineteenth century, each with a ground far above ordinary club standards and each with a supporting public far keener than is usual in ordinary villages. The district league was founded in 1891, but many of the clubs are forty or fifty years older than that. Records of the Honley club go back to 1843, the Armitage Bridge club was founded in 1848 and Holmfirth in 1850. Dalton records are available from 1831, but it is reasonably claimed that the club was founded earlier, even earlier than Lascelles Hall. Most of the other clubs came to life in the 'sixties and 'seventies, and it can be said that for nearly a hundred years cricket—good cricket—has been played on these green uplands. From this part of the West Riding it is probable that more cricketers have gone out into the world to be professionals in other leagues or play for their own or for other counties than from any other corner of England. At least eight have represented their country. As for those who have played for Yorkshire or, in Yorkshire's prodigality, have been allowed to emigrate to other counties, the number, so far as I can reckon, is sixty-five, and among these are included: from Kirkheaton, Hirst and Rhodes, first in any company in the world; from Armitage Bridge, Schofield Haigh, scarcely less illustrious; and from Paddock, Percy Holmes, hero of sixty-nine century opening partnerships with Sutcliffe, and Willie Watson, saviour of England at Lord's in 1953. But when all is said and done, the biggest battalion marches from Lascelles Hall, a battalion almost big enough to form *two* county elevens.

Over the years, down from the breezy uplands, comes the delectable sound of bat and ball; the sound of Ephraim Lockwood cutting 'em straight or of Allan Hill rattling the enemy's stumps.

" *Give me Lascelles Hall.*" So spoke Ephraim Lockwood, and a greater than he said much the same thing. One evening a good many years ago a friend of mine had to meet Sir Stanley Jackson, the great Jacker, at Huddersfield station, for the purpose of conveying him to a meeting. As they reached the outside of that classic portico, Jacker glanced round. " Tell me," he said, as if it mattered more than anything else in the world, " which would be the road to Lascelles Hall? "

When the southern folk speak patronizingly of this place as the Hambledon of the North, we northerners are unmoved. We think well of Hambledon. We should not mind if it called itself the Lascelles Hall of the South.

E 2

CHAPTER IX

PARSON'S PLEASURE

I

ONE of the most fascinating sections of Wisden is the one headed *Births and Deaths of Cricketers*. In one sense at least cricketers are like the rest of us: they are mortal. It is a 'good thing' when they are born and a sad thing when they die. But in another sense they are above the rest of us: mere mortality is not for them. Grace and Trumper died in 1915, and sad events these deaths were, heaven knows; but who shall deny to Grace and Trumper the truest immortality?

And, in a lesser sense, there is an immortality of sorts for the humblest cricketer. Even though you are no Grace or Trumper, no Hobbs or Bradman, no Hutton or Arthur Morris, so long as you are a cricketer within Wisden's broad interpretation of the word, you will not be deprived of your small share of deathless fame. You may not be Bailey, Mr. T. E. (Cambridge University, Essex and England), *b.* 1923. But, however modest your attainments may be, you will be immortalized: Blobbs, Mr. B. (Bluntshire), *b.* 1930. And there, embedded and embalmed, you will remain. Even when they reverently add: *d.* 2020, you will stay where you are for ever, or practically for ever.

When I last thumbed through *Births and Deaths* I was struck by two facts: the presence, indeed the prevalence, among its pages of clergymen of the Church of England; and the wonderful longevity of these reverend gentlemen. In the Wisden I have been looking at I found about eighty of them, and, according to my calculations, their average age was (or is) also about eighty. This seems to argue that cricketing clergymen live lives of happy contentment, with no enemy but winter and rough weather, and with the promise of May ever round the corner. They may spend fifty years doing their duty and having their fun, without any deeper sorrow than a sticky run-out and no worse frustration than a leg-before-wicket decision refused. Show me a cricketing parson and I will show you a good man and a happy man.

The Methuselah-like quality of the breed is astonishing. If I were an insurance company I would offer them specially favourable terms, as some companies favour teetotallers, with less reason. Ninety as a score in years is not infrequent, eighty is common form, and seventy would seem to be a mere opportunity for getting your second wind after some quick running between the wickets. Some of them have concluded their innings at these excellent scores, but many are still batting, moving on serenely towards their century. The nervous nineties have no terrors for them.

Was it not the Rev. W. Fellows who, while practising at Oxford, drove the longest hit ever made, 175 yards by the measuring tape, ' from hit to pitch '? It was the Rev. Vernon Royle of Lancashire, the best cover-point of his day, who was capable of perturbing the imperturbable Tom Emmett, and worthy to be named with Jessop and Hobbs. It was Canon ' Joe ' McCormick to whom Ted Pooley ruefully observed: " If he bowls straight you plays 'em, and if he bowls crooked, you clouts 'em! " It was the Rev. F. R. R. Browne who bowled for Sussex (and bowled well) with such a peculiar action that it was said by one of the Sussex professionals that he brought the ball ' out of his ear-'ole '. It was the Rev. A. P. Wickham, of Oxford and Somerset, who was keeping wicket in light brown pads and a faded Harlequin cap when W. G. Grace made his hundredth hundred. " He only let five balls pass his bat," said Wickham, " in the whole innings." And was it not the Rev. Charles Kingsley who played cricket with the boys of Eversley on Sunday afternoons, but sternly denied an innings to those who had not been to church in the morning?

Who was the first of these reverend cricketers? Certainly the first famous one was the Rev. Lord Frederick Beauclerk, who dominated the field of play in his time as Grace and

Bradman did in theirs. Born in 1773, the son of the Duke of
St. Albans, he was descended from Charles II and Mistress
Eleanor Gwyn, and there is no doubt that in his nature he drew
distinction, charm and a certain wilful *naughtiness* from ancestors
so distinguished in their own field. He was almost the most
famous member the M.C.C. ever had. He was vicar of Kimp-
ton and St. Michaels, St. Albans, but at no time in his life was
he crippled by the burdens of pastoral care. Most of his time he
spent at Lord's, whether as an eager player or, in later life,
as an equally keen spectator. In both of these roles he was a
martinet. He was first seen bowling at Cambridge in 1790,
and brought up to Lord's to play in the ' great ' matches.
There were, of course, no university games and no regular
county matches, but the M.C.C. games were frequent and All
England sides were continually in action.

Lord Frederick was a slow bowler, full of tricks, who would
tempt the batsman in a most unecclesiastical way; by some
uncanny prescience he knew your favourite stroke and would
set a fieldsman to block it. Like a good many bowlers before
and since, he did not enjoy being hit and still less did he enjoy
the contemplation of a batsman who played him with a dead
bat. When that ' unadulterated rustic ', Tom Walker of
Hambledon, blocked his first four balls, playing him with
coolness and ease, he grew furious and, as was his custom when
' disappointed ', dashed down his tall white hat upon the
ground.

"You confounded old beast!" cried his Reverend Lord-
ship.

But old Tom chuckled.

" I doan't care what he says." And the tall white hat must
have been dashed down again several times before Tom's
innings was ended.

As a batsman, Lord Frederick was a model of the classical
school; indeed, he must have been one of the founding fathers
of the style: upright stance, left leg well forward and a rich
repertory of flashing strokes on the off. Just as J. T. Tyldesley
was the only professional who could hold his own in an England

side among the magnificent galaxy of amateurs at the beginning
of the twentieth century, so Lord Frederick Beauclerk was the
only amateur to play regularly for All England a hundred years
earlier.

Our cricketing parsons are, as a body, probably the most
virtuous bunch of human beings that ever existed in a far from
perfect world, but, lest one good custom should corrupt the
world, here is one who was by no means narrowly virtuous.
Lord Frederick took a broad view of the possibilities of financial
gain on the cricket field, and boasted that he made £600 a year
by bets on the game. Like some later great figures, he did not
like being out; he did not like not getting wickets when he
was bowling; and he did not like the side on which he was
playing to lose. Within reason, he was right, but he often went
beyond reason. Nevertheless, like Chesterton's drunkard's,
his sins they are forgiven him, for he was a very great
cricketer.

There is one record of how he might have won a match if only
he could have kept his temper. A single-wicket match was
arranged: on one side Lord Frederick and T. C. Howard, a
famous bowler, and on the other 'Squire' Osbaldeston, along
with William Lambert, the best-known Surrey player, and
indeed the most eminent professional, of the period. On the
day, Osbaldeston was ill, and naturally made an attempt to
postpone the match, but Lord Frederick, no doubt scenting an
easy victory, insisted like Shylock on the letter of the law,
and demanded that play should begin. Osbaldeston, who
knew that he would be a complete passenger, staggered to the
wicket in the hope of scoring one run, thereby being able to
claim a substitute in the field. He scored his single, but,
Shylock again intervening, was refused his substitute. In spite
of everything, however, the cunning and resourceful Lambert,
his confidence unimpaired, went in and made a cocky 56.
Lord Frederick had to go in for the last innings to 'win or lose
it all', but he found he was facing a character as full of guile as
himself. Lambert bowled wides, which did not at that period
of cricket history count against him, until Lord Frederick grew

so furious that he lashed out, gave a c. and b. and lost the match by 15 runs. And what reward Lambert received from ' Squire ' Osbaldeston's family is nobody's business.

Though this game was lost, Lord Frederick won many single-wicket matches. He made eight centuries at the old Lord's ground on what is now Dorset Square. As ruler and legislator in the pavilion, his influence was powerful and, despite his gambling propensities, normally on the side of the angels. He did many things that would not be countenanced in these mild and well-ordered times, and by his imperious manner— was he not the fourth son of a Duke and the best gentleman-player of his time?—he made many enemies, some of whom whispered in corners that he did unspeakable things. It is more probable, however, that his good name has suffered more from his high-handedness than from his positive sins. He did not often grossly break the rules, but merely, using the great force and authority of his character and position, interpreted them in a light favourable to himself. And if he made enemies among rival amateurs and disgruntled professionals, he could be genial towards the young. He was even known to tip a guinea to a couple of schoolboys who took his wicket at practice. He was making hundreds in his fifties, and in his last Gentlemen *v.* Players match in 1835 he played a majestic innings, comparable only with W. G. Grace's swan-song in 1906.

There are two final pictures of him which remain in the memory. One shows him as the keen critic, puffing his cigar and frowning while his little dog barked at the batsmen as they came and went. The other is one of those ' sad stories of the death of kings '. It has more than a touch of pathos, and shows him in his old age, his playing days long finished, leaning back in his brougham on the boundary's edge at Lord's, his nurse beside him, watching intently the kingdom he had ruled so long and whose crown he must soon resign. . . .

Some of the cricketing parsons were chroniclers, as for example the Rev. John Mitford, who wrote a glowing review of Nyren's *Young Cricketer's Tutor* in the *Gentleman's Magazine* of July and September 1833. His description of a fine summer

morning on Broad Halfpenny Down brings a catch of the breath
even to an unrepentant supporter of Lascelles Hall.

> "You know the scenery of that secluded vale; the fine undulating
> sweep of the beechen forests, the beautiful and variegated turf, the
> glittering of the ocean, the blue hills of the Isle of Wight looming in
> the distance, and the elmy gardens and half wild orchards sprinkled
> in the bottom."

Another noted chronicler was the Rev. James Pycroft, who
in 1837 made a passionate pilgrimage in search of the life-stories
of the Hambledon men and, in particular, of William (Silver
Billy) Beldham, that 'tottering silver-haired old man', and
other worthies of cricket's first famous generation. Beldham
liked to see a player 'upright and well forward to face the
ball like a man '. When he described a match arranged by the
Duke of Dorset between the Old Players and the New, he
smiled ruefully. "You laugh, sir," he said, "but we were all
New once. . . ."

A Yorkshire parson-cricketer of whom I heard much in my
boyhood was the Rev. E. S. Carter, who was then Vicar of
St. Michael-le-Belfry, York. He was born in 1845 and lived, a
good and happy man, until he was seventy-eight. He was,
like all of them except Lord Frederick, a conscientious parson
before he was a cricketer, and he never turned out for his
county as often as he or they would have liked. He took his
holidays at the time of the Scarborough Festival, and he also
played a lot of mid-week cricket for Yorkshire Gentlemen, in his
day a formidable side. When he was vicar-choral in York
Minster he was able to convert to the true faith a particularly
gloomy Dean, who had disapproved of his playing so much
cricket. During service Carter found himself solemnly bearing
towards the altar a heavy silver tray on which a pile of offertory
bags had been carelessly heaped. To his dismay he saw from
the corner of his eye that one of the bags was slipping earth-
wards. Instantly he shot out his right hand, brilliantly fielding
the bag and at the same time balancing the tray on his left.
Honour was saved, the offertory was reverently preserved and
the Dean never said a word against cricket for the rest of his life.

Mr. Carter, too, was a noted preacher, after-dinner speaker and story-teller. Uncle Walter said he was the finest speaker he had ever heard except Lord Rosebery. (Uncle Walter always used Lord Rosebery as his standard of the superlative in oratory. He would no more have taken Mr. Gladstone's name in vain by comparison with the mortal and fallible than he would have appealed to the Deity in a minor matter.) The Rev. E. S. Carter, my uncle said, had a better selection of cricket stories than anybody he had ever known. Half the cricketing-parson stories were originally told by or about him. The story about Crossland and the parson has been told about every cricketing parson who ever played, but it really happened to Mr. Carter. Crossland, an essentially rugged Lancashire type, noted for sulphurous language, was warned that a clergyman was approaching the wicket. While Carter was rattling up a merry forty, Crossland said nothing, but when he hit the parson's stumps with a very fast ball, he let out an untheological yell: " That's downed his old pulpit for him! " But, as Sammy Woods used to say, that wasn't the way Archie MacLaren used to tell the story.

E. S. Carter was brought up under old Parson Trueman—not Fred, an unlikely candidate for Holy Orders—whose idea of a grace before or after meals was to exclaim ' Play ' or ' Over '. Winning a scholarship to Oxford, Carter was one of the few genuine double Blues who both played in the University eleven and rowed in the University boat. (Canon ' Joe ' McCormick was another.) Not merely did Carter do this but he nearly killed himself in the process. One day he dashed off from the lecture-room to practise with his partner for the ' Varsity Pairs ', rowed over the course twice, dashed back to the College cricket ground, took seven wickets, made a not-out century, retired in a thunderstorm, tore back to the Isis to row in his heat in a college ' scratch four ', won his heat, rowed in another, ran back to college in another thunderstorm. His doctor (with the assistance of pleurisy) kept him in bed for three weeks and then sent him off to Australia. This deprived him of his third cricket and rowing Blues, but it gave him a chance, through an accidental meeting with a friend on landing at Melbourne, to play in an inter-State match (they called it an inter-Colonial match then) for Victoria against New South Wales. The hard hitting by which he made top score in each innings brought victory to Victoria, and for the rest of his short stay he was subjected to a hero-worship which he bore with modest amusement.

Back in England, he was ordained and became a curate in Ealing. There, as an intelligible part of his pastoral work, he helped old Tom Hearne to found the Ealing cricket club. Once, before a match against a strong Surrey side, brought down by our old friend Ted Pooley, Carter had to be absent owing to some clerical duty but, receiving an S.O.S. message from Tom Hearne that a massacre was in progress, dashed over to the ground, put up a tremendous bowling performance and saw his side through to victory by 15 runs. Pooley's comment was characteristic: " Tell you what, Tom. Next time we'll play you on Sunday, when that chap's safe in church."

Not many cricketers, even clerical cricketers, are noted both as wicket-keepers and fast bowlers. Carter was both, and not only was he a highly successful fast bowler in his youth; he was also, as he grew older, a deceptive purveyor of slow lobs. *Tiddleywinks*, they were derisively called, but they all too frequently got their man. When he returned northwards to his native county he performed prodigies of bowling valour. It almost seems from the records that he could not take his surplice off without doing the hat-trick. He thought nothing of taking nine wickets—nine for 9, seven for 9, seven for 8 and seven for 2 : these little episodes were meat and drink to him. Later in life he took to wicket-keeping and again he showed high genius. Somewhere around the age of fifty he was indulging in feats of wicket-keeping comparable to his extraordinary bouts of bowling. Playing in a match for Yorkshire Gentlemen, this elderly clergyman claimed seven victims, three of them being stumped off successive balls. Despite these slightly staggering feats, he always claimed two of his actions were more valuable to cricket than anything else. One was the recruiting of the famous Yorkshire and England slow bowler, Ted Peate, the spiritual ancestor of Peel, Rhodes and Verity, through picking him up to play for a side that had come short of a man. The other thing of which Carter was most proud was the fact that he was the first to invite Lord (then the Hon. Martin Bladen) Hawke to play for Yorkshire at Scarborough. The following year Hawke took his place in the eleven, and in 1883, at the end of the Varsity term, he became captain. The path of duty was the way to glory.

2

I have to confess that my favourite cricketer-parson was not of my own county. He played for the modest county in which I lived later for fifteen years, and his name was the Rev. F. H. Gillingham. For me he was the ideal cricketing parson: a happy, kindly person and a splendid performer. As a man, he was a gentle soul, and yet, as a batsman, his driving was as the driving of Jehu, son of Nimshi, for he drove furiously. It was as if he loved the whole world, but, so that he might not claim greater nobility than the rest of the frail human race, he preserved one modicum of anger which he vented upon a small red ball which he dismissed with almost divine wrath to the boundary. There was a touch of the Old Testament in the way in which he smote them hip and thigh with great slaughter.

Gillingham was a devout and devoted clergyman, and he rarely had the leisure to play the cricket that he loved; when he snatched a day or two to help Essex he came in without much practice and succeeded by sheer ' optimism and enterprise '. As a lad he was in the eleven at Dulwich, that school of fine cricketers, among whom were Trevor Bailey, S. C. Griffith, Hugh Bartlett, the Gilligans and (don't forget) P. G. Wodehouse. As an undergraduate at Durham University, too, Gillingham compiled some huge scores. His connection with Essex began with his appointment as a curate at Leyton, an ideal parish for a cricketing parson. At the very most, he could never manage to appear in more than half the county's programme. Whenever he played, Essex was stronger in batting, fielding and morale. In 1904 he hit up a tornado of a double century against Middlesex at Lord's (the right place for tornadoes); in 1908 he made a series of big scores and compiled 1,000 runs during the comparatively short time he was able to play; and in the same year he turned out for the Gentlemen against the Players, the first clergyman to do so since 1859.

From 1910 till the outbreak of the First World War he was in Birmingham; he then came for nine years to Bermondsey, where the young folk never had a finer leader; after that he had seventeen years at St. Margaret's, Lee, Blackheath. Everywhere he worked he was greatly loved. He was a much better preacher than most muscular Christians are and, besides this, his private and personal work brought him many friends, especially among the boys and girls. Once, in Bermondsey, I heard him read the lesson on the raising of Jairus's daughter, and I remember to this day the dramatic simplicity of his voice; it conveyed, without forced pathos, the utter sadness of the death of a child.

One of his best friends said that his character was so straightforward, he disliked the guile of slow bowlers. If that was so he undoubtedly ' took it out of ' the others. The fast stuff he revelled in.

The most remarkable career among parson-cricketers is surely that of J. H. (Jack) Parsons, who began as a Warwickshire professional and is now vicar of Liskeard and an honorary canon of Truro Cathedral. Not many parsons, as we have seen, have played for the Gentlemen; only one has played for both the Gentlemen and the Players. Only four men besides J. H. Parsons, have played for both sides; E. J. Diver, another Warwickshire man, the great Richard Daft, W. R. Hammond, and W. J. Edrich. Like Gillingham, Parsons was tall and powerful. Before the First World War he had already become a Warwickshire pro, and, when hostilities began was beginning to make a name for himself as a hard-hitting batsman. Serving in the war in the Indian Army, he won the

Military Cross and returned to England in 1923 with the rank
of captain. Resigning his commission, he again played for
some years as a professional and distinguished himself by big
hitting and fine slip-fielding.

Later he studied at St. Aidan's, was ordained in 1929 and
took up his first curacy at Rugby, where he served for four
years.

One of his finest innings was a score of 161 for Warwickshire
at Edgbaston against the West Indian touring side in 1928.
In this he hit four sixes off successive balls. The fourth hit a
cup of tea which was being held by a lady standing beside the
sight-screen; with the accuracy of a surgical operation the cup
was removed from the handle, which remained in the lady's
hand. The operation was also painless. The whole thing
must have seemed like a mysterious atomic explosion seventeen
years before its time. An earlier feat of fast scoring was
achieved in 1924, when he took part in a partnership of 392
in less than four hours against Sussex.

In his Gentlemen v. Players matches he played for the
Players in 1914, in 1925 (when he hit up a fierce 72) and 1927;
his appearances for the Gentlemen were in 1929, 1930 and
1931. In the 1930 match his most valuable contribution was
not his hard-hit 57, but his five catches, four of them taken
in a succession of positions varying from long-off to mid-on.
In each of these games he was a good man, in every sense of
the word, to have on the side. One of the happiest matches he
ever played in was also one of his last. In 1934 he carried
Warwickshire to a thrilling win over Yorkshire at Scarborough.
In the first innings Warwickshire had been hurled out for 45,
but, mainly through a wonderful 94 by Parsons, which contained
twelve fours and three sixes, they scraped through by one
wicket. When at the beginning of the 1939–45 war he finally
settled down in a vicarage, he chose a minor county, but I
should think that Cornwall never could allow itself to be called
a minor county once the Rev. J. H. Parsons had gone to live
there.

3

The one tragic exception to the placid rule of long life among cricketing parsons was the death of the Rev. E. T. Killick at the age of forty-six. While still at St. Paul's he played for a public schools eleven against the 1926 Australian touring side, and when he went up to Cambridge he showed the quality of an England batsman. Coming from school with a high reputation, he played for Cambridge in 1928, making top score (74) in the first innings of a Varsity match that was drawn, but excitingly so. Cambridge had the heavier metal, but the last two Oxford men hung on by their eyebrows till seven o'clock, at which hour Sir Pelham Warner had almost gnawed through the handle of his umbrella. Killick batted well in 1929, but it was in 1930 that he showed his superlative value. His duel with Peebles, the spearhead of the Oxford attack, was a battle of giants about which connoisseurs talk in wet-windowed pavilions to this day. The batsman's stubborn resistance undoubtedly enabled a comparatively weak Cambridge to beat an undeniably strong Oxford.

In 1928 Killick played in the light-hearted Gentlemen v. Players match at Folkestone and did quite well, and in 1929 he batted splendidly at Lord's against a strong Players' eleven in which Freeman was the menacing bowler. In the same year he was one of several Cambridge players to turn out for Middlesex, and he made a dashing 170 against Sussex and 140 against Essex. In 1929 he played twice in Tests against the visiting South African team and had the honour of going in first for England with Sutcliffe. In the only championship game in which he was able to turn out in 1931 he scored a double century, a tribute to his fitness and concentration.

During the war he served as chaplain with the R.A.F. in West Africa and afterwards became vicar of Bishop's Stortford, where he was greatly loved as a padre and as a man. While playing in a diocesan cricket match between the clergy of St. Albans and Coventry he collapsed at the wicket and died on his way to hospital. It is always a tragedy when a man dies young, particularly a man of fine character and wide influence for good.   But, if a good man must die young, it is conceivable that he might choose to die pursuing the most innocent of pleasures among the friends he loves.

I do not know when D. S. Sheppard, of Cambridge University, Sussex and England, intends to take Holy Orders, but I fear when he does his friends will see very little more of him on the cricket-field.   As a cricketer he has had a career of almost unbroken success.   In his last year at Sherborne he had an average of nearly 80; he did his military service before going up to Cambridge, and in the meantime made three centuries for Sussex; three times he played in the Varsity match, captaining his side and making a century in 1952; in the match against the West Indies in 1950 he shared with Dewes, another prolific scorer, a record Cambridge first-wicket partnership of 343. He was not very successful in his Australian tour of 1950–51 and did not play against South Africa on his return, but in 1952 he was selected for two Tests, and in the Oval game made a century.   That year he and his Cambridge friend, Peter May, headed the country's first-class batting averages with 64 and 62 respectively.   Indeed, there are shrewd critics who say that, among the several tried, he might well have been Hutton's ideal opening partner.   In 1953 he was Sussex's friendly but forceful captain, putting the side in better heart than it had enjoyed since the happy days of A. E. R. Gilligan.   (What do *you* think, Arthur?)

It should be legitimate to hope, without impertinence, that he will spare as much time as possible for cricket.   It may be that he will carry out his early wish to become a missionary; whatever he does will be governed by firm character and conscience.   But I hope he will not cease to be among those to whom cricket is parson's pleasure.

CHAPTER X

COMMONWEALTH OF CRICKET

I

THERE are one or two things which the countries of the
Commonwealth have in common. Above all, there is the
noble and gracious institution of monarchy. There is also the
odd thing called the democratic way of life, which, if looked on
without sententiousness, has certain merits. The virtues of
tolerance and good humour go along with them, and with
them also goes the game of cricket, for which I would in the
first instance make no higher claim than that it has caused a
great deal of pleasure to flow round the world and has enabled
an exceedingly large number of citizens of one Commonwealth
country to have an equally large circle of friends in another.

In how many countries have Sir Pelham Warner and Sir
Jack Hobbs got friends? The number must be very large
indeed. A man like Patsy Hendren is known and loved
wherever he has played. On every ground of every Commonwealth country he was always a prime favourite with the crowd,
who invariably chipped him boisterously, though, to do him
justice, whenever he was ragged from the ring he gave as good
as he got. But the friendship that cricket fosters is not merely
among the eminent; it is to a great extent a friendship between
peoples. Since the middle of the nineteenth century teams
from England have visited Australia, South Africa, Canada,
the United States (not a Commonwealth country, but you
never know), New Zealand, the West Indies, India and Pakistan. South Africa, India and the West Indies visit Australia.
Australia and New Zealand visit South Africa. India has
toured the West Indies. Mixed ' Dominion ' teams have toured
India under the managership of George Duckworth, and have
contained Englishmen, Australians, West Indians and others
of whom nothing is asked except that they should be cricketers.

151

Nor is that all. The universities have led, at least since Ranji's time, in welcoming first-class Commonwealth cricketers in their elevens. Duleepsinhji, the Nawab of Pataudi, R. H. Bettington, H. G. Owen-Smith, Clive Van Ryneveld—these are only a few of the well-known names. The Oxford team that won the exciting Varsity match of 1946 contained four Commonwealth players. Each year more of these visitors appear in English county sides, and in 1953 there were Commonwealth players who stood high in the batting and bowling averages, including the only one who did ' the double '. There are admittedly two ways of looking at this question, and there are some who shake their heads over it, muttering about thin ends and wedges. But not every county is sufficiently rich and well-populated to insist, like Yorkshire, on a hard-and-fast birth qualification. Some counties in the lower-income group have placed themselves on an even financial keel through the acquisition of a talented Commonwealth player. In any event, I should hate not to have watched players of the quality of Livingston, Tribe, Dooland or Walsh.

A thought that gives me continuous pleasure is the reflection that, walking the streets of crowded towns in Lancashire, there are dark-skinned heroes who on summer Saturdays will be knocking up fifties and taking six wickets, to the delight of the local citizenry. I will wager that Nelson did its duty the better for the knowledge that Learie Constantine was its immensely energetic professional, and that more recently that hearts have been higher in Haslingden because Vinoo Mankad could be relied on to give his attractive weekly all-round performances.

I would not, I say, make too high a claim for the game. Commonwealth cricket has done wonders, but it has not performed the ultimate miracle. This will occur when South Africa invites a team of West Indians or Indians to visit its shores. When that happens I shall come nearer to dying happy. But even up to now there are people in every Commonwealth country who have, without the consciousness of virtue, contrived to spread a band of light across the world.

2

Victor Trumper was loved by gods and men and died young. For those who saw him even once he is an abiding memory. For the present generation the greatest name in Australian, perhaps in any, cricket is Bradman. That is fair and right, and his doings were prodigious. But for those of us who are older the great Australian name is Trumper. If cricket history had to be reduced to half a dozen names, which heaven forbid, Trumper would still be one of them. Some are great by dominance and by colossal achievement, as were W. G. Grace and Sir Donald Bradman; some live by having been rich comedy characters, as were Tom Emmett and Happy Jack Ulyett. (I have already said that Johnny Wardle is rapidly qualifying for this status.) There have been others, a rare and happy few, whose immortality lives in sheer brilliance, and among these are Ranji, Jessop and, not least, Victor Trumper. To this brilliance in the technique of batsmanship Trumper added a personal charm that went far deeper than charm usually goes, and a genuine kindness of heart, not so much rare among cricketers as rare among the whole human race.

It has been said of Victor Trumper that his cricket was as noble as his character; his style was the very poetry of motion. In the famous Fry and Beldam book of photographs is a picture—in my opinion the finest of all those fine pictures—of Trumper leaping out to drive. It is a picture that shows in him the perfection of natural easy grace. His strokes did not seem to have violence, yet the ball fled to the boundary with the speed of light. His off-drive was a thing of beauty; his late-cut was almost a caress. He was a magician in the sense that Ranji was a magician, though not quite so fantastic; his foot-work was so remarkable that often, when he had sent the ball to the pickets at scorching speed, he appeared to have played it with a lazy swing. I have seen Hammond appear to do this kind of thing, too, through perfect timing, but Trumper seemed to attain an even higher standard of perfection. The sheer grace of the stroke concealed its power. C. G. Macartney, the only other man besides Trumper and Bradman who ever made a century in a Test before lunch, said of a particular hit of his at Sydney:

> "A yorker from Laver was the ball he selected for the hit, and with no apparent effort he seemed to pick it up with the bat, and it finished on the roof of the northern pavilion at straight hit. I have seen bigger hits made by lunging, but this was a fast-footed one, necessitated by the pitch of the ball."

He made all the bowling look easier than it was, and those who played with him said he had three or four strokes to every ball. When you watched him, it seemed as if each ball was exactly the right one to hit. Of his forty-two centuries, six of them against England, many were scored on wicked wickets against bowling of immaculate length. His innings on rain-ruined pitches were almost incomparable. In a critical phase of a vital Test on a vile wicket he would bat with a gay gallantry that the ordinary player of to-day would hardly dare display at Scarborough Festival. His 74 in the second Test at Melbourne in 1903–04 was probably one of the best in the history of the game, only surpassed, if it was surpassed, by J. T. Tyldesley's 62 in the same game. (That is why I said 'almost' incomparable. It is inevitable that Trumper and the Tyldesley of that tour should be compared.) Once the wicket had reached its worst, nobody else made any runs at all. In the same series, in the previous Test at Sydney, he had played another of his most dashing innings. After a classic duel with Wilfred Rhodes, who on a batsman's wicket took five wickets (but not Trumper's) for 94, he made a glorious 185 not out. Towards the end of the day he said to the bowler: "Just a little bit of mercy, Wilfred; just one loose ball. . . ." But he never received one in the whole innings.

In 1905–06, against Victoria, also on a sticky wicket, Trumper made 101 out of 139 in fifty-seven minutes, and a year later on an equally hostile pitch he repeated his triumph with 119 out of 150 in 101 minutes. It was almost impossible to bowl a length to him and quite impossible, when he was in his highest form, to set a field for him. Eleven men were not

enough. Some cricketers have had genuine greatness in the
orthodox manner, as had Hobbs and Fry. Some, a rare but
happy few, delight us by sheer magic: Ranji, Jessop, Trumper.
Others abide our question, but there is no analysis for enchantment.

To say that the man was as charming as his cricket is a poor
kind of praise. Often we call a pleasant individual charming
because we cannot think of anything else to say of him. Sometimes we use the word charm to denote qualities which are
amiable but superficial. But once in a generation, or even less
often, comes a man whose charm springs from deep kindness of
heart. It may have some element of serenity in unmatched
skill; it certainly goes with an unsententious love of a man's
fellows, not of some windy abstraction called humanity, but of
the individuals with whom he lives, works and plays. Nobility
of character, like Trumper's, is rare in Australia or anywhere
else. There is so often in your Australian a native truculence,
and good luck to it, which I would not for an instant criticize,
or wish to change. Bradman had it, Barnes had it, and
O'Reilly was not called 'Tiger' for nothing. It is legitimate
and right, though perhaps Australia has a little too much of it,
just as England has too little. Trumper's kindness of heart
brought him ill-luck in business. (I suspect that he used to
drop his prices to an uneconomic level for those who he did not
think could afford the right price.) When the quarrels that
preceded Australia's tour to England in 1912 were at their
bitterest, he was on the side of the players, because he believed
them to be right in principle, but in a dispute in which practically every inhabitant of the continent was hurling impreca-
tions at every other inhabitant, not a single harsh word was said
by or to Victor Trumper.

His testimonial match in 1912 was the most famous in
Australian cricket history, except, of course, Bradman's. When
Trumper went in to bat, the emotional disturbance among the
cheering crowd was so great that when he essayed to hit the
first ball sent down to him, by immemorial custom a long hop
on the leg side, he missed it. The sigh of relief that greeted its

safe arrival in the wicket-keeper's gloves could be heard all over
Sydney. If Trumper had been bowled, either the umpire
would have given him not out or the crowd would have
lynched the bowler. But all was well, and Trumper went on to
make one of the most dashing centuries of his career.

When he died in 1915, all Sydney was in mourning, and the
inhabitants of that far from sentimental city felt that they had
lost a close friend. In the memory of those who saw him he
remains in a series of mental pictures which show him cutting as
with the angel's flaming sword or dancing for ever down the
pitch to drive a ball off the earth. It is not fantastic to think
of Keats, who died young of the same cruel disease, surveying
on his Grecian Urn the ' fair youth beneath the trees. . . .'
That is how Victor Trumper lives, eternally young, eternally
gay, eternally a noble artist. He never grew old.

3

After Australia, South Africa. The first Test match between
England and South Africa was played in 1888–89 and splendidly
fought contests have taken place at intervals ever since. The
last three series have given victory to England, but I have a
South African friend who assures me that the next touring side
from his country to visit these damp shores will give England a
thrashing. Because of their youth and fanatical fitness they
can bat as well, bowl as well and field, he says, a dashed sight
better than any eleven England can put into the field. These
are the lads who did so brilliantly in Australia in 1952–53.
For us, in England, it is always Australia who is the beloved
enemy and, this being so, it is odd that two of England's
greatest captains should each have stated that his own finest
and tensest Test was played against South Africa: Sir Pelham
Warner's at Johannesburg in 1905–06, when England lost by
one wicket, and C. B. Fry's at Leeds in 1907, when England
won by 53 runs making a fighting recovery after having been
flung out for 76, mainly through superb bowling by Aubrey
Faulkner.

Who has been South Africa's greatest player? As we know,

there are fine youngsters coming along, and those who reached their prime a little while ago, such as Dudley Nourse and Eric Rowan, were very good indeed. But going back to 'my' time, I think most contemporary players and spectators would agree that the king of South African batsmen was 'Herbie' Taylor, who had something of the classic quality of MacLaren, touched with an occasional dash of Trumper, in his power of repeatedly getting away an 'impossible' ball. He was one of the few batsmen in the world who have even mastered Sydney Barnes. He played, between the years 1912 and 1932, in a larger number of Tests than any South African except David Nourse, and only two have had a higher batting average than his, which was over 40.

But model of batting magnificence as Taylor was, I would choose somebody else as a symbol of South African cricket. There is one name that is at the same time even more brilliant and more characteristic. Seldom has any country produced a more versatile all-rounder than Aubrey Faulkner. Averages are not everything, but over a period of nearly twenty years they are a reasonable guide. In Tests between 1906 and 1924 he was always doing something outstanding with bat and ball; he was near the top of the averages in both. His batting figure was a tiny decimal higher than Herbert Taylor's and only one man took more wickets or paid less for them.

In a way the curve of his career was not unlike that of the great Wilfred Rhodes: he began as a bowler, became very nearly the greatest all-rounder of his period; then he shone even more as a batsman. In that story-book match in which MacLaren's 'young men' conquered the unconquerable Australian eleven of 1921, it was Faulkner's matchless innings of 153 that turned the scale. And before the end of his career he was again bowling splendidly. He played against the 1905–06 English touring side, and came over with the splendid 1907 side, which contained, or so it seemed to harassed English batsmen, almost all the googly bowlers in the world. England had one Bosanquet; South Africa had five. There can never have been such a menacing array: G. A. Faulkner, A. E.

Vogler, R. O. Schwartz, S. J. Snooke and G. C. White. In 1909–10 Faulkner once more performed prodigiously in his own country against the English touring side.   In each match of the five he made at least 50 and took five wickets, finishing with what was then a Test series record of 545 runs and twenty-nine wickets.   Several batsmen have made more runs and half a dozen bowlers have taken more wickets, but I doubt if there is a better series record for an all-rounder.   In 1910–11 he went with a South African side to Australia, and there made a more striking impression than any previous visiting batsman except MacLaren and Ranji.   In the Test series he scored 732 runs, another record, surpassing even Trumper, who was then in tremendous form.   Only Bradman, Hammond and Sutcliffe have beaten this.   Faulkner seemed to be able to do everything he wished in the way he wished and to do it serenely.   I have already spoken of his superb display in MacLaren's 'Young Amateurs' match.   He was thirty-nine years old, and at this point must have touched the high-water mark of his career, for he did not accomplish a great deal for South Africa's visiting team of 1924.   In the cricket school which he started in London he was as successful a coach as he had been an all-round player, and many noted young amateurs were trained under his hand. Like Trumper, he died comparatively young, but even more tragically, for he died by his own hand.   Peace be with him. He was a very great cricketer.

4

Blue sky, brazen sun and brown ' village green ': these form the background against which West Indian cricketers play. Their pitches are a batsman's heaven and a bowler's hell. Their spectators form a mass of eager, laughing, chattering humanity, crammed into every nook and cranny of the ground, swinging from the trees like monkeys.   The players are equally eager, impulsive, dashing in attack;   triumphant in victory, perhaps not so firm-footed when faced with disaster, but, at any rate, a formidable opposition at home or abroad.   The visiting West Indies side of 1950 produced three batsmen, Worrell,

Weekes and Walcott, and two bowlers, ' those little pals of mine, Ramadhin and Valentine ', who made the England of the period look small. Apart from this quick-firing quintet, there have been fine West Indian players: batsmen like C. A. Ollivierre, G. Challenor and George Headley, probably the greatest of them all, and bowlers like E. A. Martindale and C. R. Browne.

Despite the eminence of these names, they do not include the one which, when West Indies cricket is mentioned, springs most readily to the mind. That name, of course, is Constantine. The fire, the dash, the bounding vitality of the Islands are happily symbolized by that name, whose owner, it seemed, could hit a little harder, bowl a little faster, leap to catch a little higher or wider, than it would have appeared possible to the ordinary mortal to do. Born in Trinidad in 1902, Learie Nicholas Constantine was the son of a member of the very first West Indies side to tour England—a good side, but not yet raised to Test match status. Learie became a lawyer's clerk at fifteen and a civil servant at twenty-one, but his heart was in cricket. His first visit to England was in 1928, and between then and the end of his career he played all over the Commonwealth: Australia, New Zealand, India, not to mention America. From the moment English cricket-watchers saw him he became a special favourite of theirs. Perhaps more than all the players they had ever seen, he seemed continuously to have in mind the scriptural injunction: *Whatsoever thy hand findeth to do, do it with all thy might.*

When he bowled he bounded up to the crease, as though determined to shatter the stumps in several pieces, and he would follow up the ball in a menacing manner so that, even if you were lucky enough to stop it from hitting your wicket, as likely as not you would be caught at silly point or short leg *by the bowler.* When he batted, he could not wait for the ball to come to him, but would go down the pitch to hit it as though he were determined that their acquaintance should cease from that instant. He is the only player who has ever hit a ball from Eddie Gilbert, the last of the great aboriginal fast bowlers, out of the Brisbane ground, and when you remember that Eddie

Gilbert once knocked the bat clean out of Bradman's hand, you can imagine that hitting him out of the ground was not child's play. As for Constantine's fielding, he had the knack of appearing to be in two or three places at once, cutting down the crime of run stealing to a minimum.

For eight years he was professional with the Nelson club in the Lancashire League. They were, I think, a happy eight years for Nelson. It is unlikely that there has ever been a more popular professional in Lancashire League cricket, that highly organized and concentrated form of sport, which might have been invented specially to display the Constantine talents of lightning bowling, tremendous hitting and electric fielding. Maybe there was a touch of showmanship in this, but why not? As a public entertainer of the most delightful kind he was well entitled to be a showman if he wished. On the occasions when I have seen him in matches with West Indian touring sides or representative games, I have always thought of him, not as showing off, but as enjoying himself hugely. It was as if he bowled, batted and fielded with every tingling nerve and muscle from the top of his head to the tips of his fingers and toes. His enjoyment was infectious. Perhaps the man had electric current in his veins. At any rate, the pleasure he obviously took in every stroke and ball was instantaneously conveyed to every spectator round the ring. Perhaps in England we are too self-conscious or never sufficiently carefree to be exuberant but we can, on the cricket-field, enjoy the carefree exuberance of others. There is even perhaps a touch of envy in our enjoyment. I believe it is the custom on West Indian grounds to greet each joyous event, such as the dismissal of the touring side's leading batsman, with the letting off of fire-crackers. But Constantine was a human fire-cracker in himself.

Despite the light-hearted pleasure he has given to thousands, Learie Constantine has not danced easily through life. As a boy he took his cricket with infinite seriousness, practising every minute of his spare time and making a lot of spare time. His father, that excellent player, watched over young Learie's cricket with the same care which Ranji bestowed on Duleep's, but was a little more drastic in method: when young Learie dropped catches his father would box his ears. A reactionary mode, repugnant to modern educationists, but I cannot think of any player who has taken more ' impossible ' catches than Constantine.

While Constantine probably enjoyed every game he ever played, he claims that the one that gave him most delight was one of those ' Victory ' matches of 1945 in which a Dominions eleven, captained by himself, defeated an English eleven, captained by W. R. Hammond. It was a gay and absorbing struggle which at times became almost a strategic battle between the two champions, Constantine and the great Walter Hammond himself, but in the end Constantine and the Commonwealth team won in a magnificently fictional manner by 45 runs within eight minutes of time. That must have been one of the most exciting games ever played at Lord's. Martin Donnelly and Keith Miller made a century each; Hammond would not be satisfied with less than two; and every one of those hundreds was a beauty. There was a wealth of fine bowling by Wright, Hollies and Pepper, and some fielding by Constantine which had in it an element of black magic itself.

It is a paradox that some of the gayest cricket ever known was played under the strain and shadow of war. It seemed that cricket was the link with the golden days of the past and, if Providence would only be kind enough, with the golden days of the future. This match, which gave rapture to the Lord's spectators, themselves mostly in uniform, proved that cricket, symbol of many good things they had fought for, was, above all things, alive.

Besides his obvious ambitions to make the biggest hit, bowl the fastest ball and hold the craziest catch, Constantine has had one other: that is, by precept and example, to further the interests and raise the status of his coloured fellow-citizens in Britain. To this task he has addressed himself with all the fire and sincerity that he gave to his batting and bowling. And in it he has been highly successful.

F

5

Every summer my daughter and I go to Lord's for the University match. Our second object is to see some good cricket, and we are seldom disappointed. Our third object is to count the parsons walking round the roped-off pitch at lunch-time. This never fails to please; a bishop counts six and a dean four, with three (all run) for a rural one. It may be argued that a rural dean has no distinguishing habiliments, but we lived in the country for a very long time and can tell by instinct when a dean is truly rural. Our first object, I confess, is to see Oxford win, and this, to our great joy, has sometimes happened. Oxford's most convincing victory after the war was in 1946, and that, we felt, was to a great extent the work of one man, Martin Paterson Donnelly, who, when few of his colleagues were achieving anything in particular, scored 142 and seemed to halve his opponents' score by the menace of his fielding at cover.

It is an odd thing that New Zealand's two greatest batsmen, Bert Sutcliffe and Martin Donnelly, have been left-handers, but I think it is arguable that of the two Donnelly was both the more graceful and the more powerful. Though slightly on the short side, he was beautifully proportioned, with powerful shoulders. Anything that was of less than a length received ruthless punishment. Born during the First World War, he played, while a schoolboy, against E. R. T. Holmes's touring team. He was still a mere stripling when he came over to England in 1937 but, despite his youth, his selection was justified by his success: he was second in the side's batting averages for the tour and did reasonably well in Tests. After the tour he returned to take up his studies at Canterbury University College, and did not become a familiar figure on an English cricket field again until he turned up at Lord's seven years later. He was now a major in the New Zealand forces, in which he had served with distinction, and he celebrated his return to head-quarters with a punishing century in the dramatic ' Dominions match ', at which we have already glanced through the bright eyes of Learie Constantine.

Donnelly stayed on to go up to Worcester College, Oxford, where he proved himself to be the University's finest all-round athlete since the days of the great Owen-Smith. Cricket was not his only game. At rugger he played with thrust, imagination and tremendous dash at either centre-three-quarter or stand-off half and just as, in the cricket match of 1946, he seemed to win the game almost off his own bat, so in Oxford's unbeaten season of 1946–47 he almost won the Varsity rugger match off his own boot, by a sensational drop-goal at the critical moment.

His cricket was free, dashing and always delightful to watch. His fielding was as admirable as his batting, and to watch him through a summer afternoon at cover-point was to recognize a fieldsman in the mighty tradition of Jessop, Hobbs and Walter Robins. Whenever and wherever he played, cricket rose, almost as a matter of course, to a more attractive level. In 1946 his never-to-be-forgotten 142 against Cambridge was only one of his six centuries. The next year he made five centuries, and these included a sparkling and almost flawless 162 not out against the Players. Then, in 1949, he was brought in to play for the New Zealand touring side and scored 206, the highest total of the tour. It would be interesting to know which of these three great centuries—all compiled at Lord's—gave Donnelly the most pleasure. In all of them you could see in him one genuine mark of the great player, which is always to have plenty of time. In at least two of those 1949 Test matches he was responsible for saving his side from defeat.

Deciding for the time being to stay in England, he played in 1948 for Warwickshire, in which year, though not quite so successful as previously, he finished the season with a marvellous double hundred for the M.C.C. against Yorkshire. He is now living in Australia and does not seem to find much time for first-class cricket. More's the pity.

There are few young cricketers who have equalled Donnelly's record of making centuries at Lord's in the University, Gentlemen v. Players and a Test match—A. P. F. Chapman is the only other I can think of—and no other has done all this with such personal charm and modesty.

6

India's two greatest cricketers, as we have seen, never played for India. The third greatest played, with qualified success, in one series. His first and finest international achievements had already been made in England's behalf. Test match status came to India rather late, although an Indian team toured England in 1911, playing a mixed programme and winning a few of their first-class matches. (There had been at least one 'missionary' tour of India by a side led by Lord Hawke nearly twenty years before.) Since real Test matches began, India have sent four touring sides to England, and each has brought with it at least one splendid batsman, including C. K. Nayudu, V. M. Merchant, V. S. Hazare and V. Mankad. Their best bowlers have been M. Nissar, Amar Singh, L. Amarnath and V. Mankad, who has as much right to be among the bowlers as among the batsmen.

The 1952 Indian touring side had some fine young players, among whom V. L. Manjrekar did extremely well, but in Tests they wilted before the bowling of Fred Trueman, and it was only Mankad who showed them how the English bowling could be hit. The first interesting point about Mankad is that he comes from the great Ranji's state, Nawanagar. Two things happened to him while he was a boy at Nawanagar High School: he received the nickname of 'Vinoo', which has stuck to him all through his life, and he was coached by the Sussex pro., A. F. Wensley. He was still at school when he had the further advantage of being 'discovered' by Duleepsinhji, who helped him in his training. By the time he was eighteen Mankad was appearing in big cricket, playing for Western States in the competition for the Ranji Trophy, India's equivalent of the Sheffield Shield or the Currie Cup, and in 1936, after Nawanagar had formed a cricket association of its own, it won the Ranji Trophy at the first time of asking, mainly through fine all-round play by Mankad.

A team captained by Lord Tennyson toured India in 1937–38 and played some unofficial Test matches: in these, through the excellence of his play, Mankad found an admirer in Tennyson himself. Later, when at the end of the war the Australian Service eleven toured India on its way home, Mankad won another admirer in Lindsay Hassett, who, laconic though he might be, opened his lips sufficiently wide to observe that Mankad was darn' good. It was on the strength of such achievements and commendations that he came to England in 1946 with the touring side brought over by the Nawab of Pataudi. Of this side Mankad was so much an integral and vertebral part that he was rested in only two matches throughout an arduous tour. Though he was not so prolific as Merchant and Hazare, or so brilliant as Pataudi, he shared in seven century stands, four of which made Indian records for the first, fourth, sixth and eighth wickets. Successful as was his business-like right-hand batting, he did even better with his slow left-arm bowling, taking well over twice as many wickets as any other bowler in the side. His inevitable ' double ' was the first achieved by a visiting player since Constantine's (also inevitable) in 1928.

Between the tours of 1946 and 1952 he had spent his English summers delighting Lancashire crowds in League cricket. In the winter of 1951–52 he played for India against a touring Pakistan side and, though he took part in only four Tests, he took twenty-five of the seventy-three wickets that fell. He also completed the Test match double of 1,000 runs and 100 wickets. (His only companions in this achievement have been George Giffen, M. A. Noble, Wilfred Rhodes and Maurice Tate.) In 1952 he was unable to play for India, except in three of the four Tests. If he had been able to play for his country right through the season, the touring side might not have had so unhappy a time, but, owing to disagreements with the Indian authorities, he could, or would, play no more. After India's defeat in the first Test at the hands of England and Fred Trueman, Mankad's services were asked for and, with Haslingden's permission, he came into the team in the second Test at Lord's. In the first innings he made 72, and after the Englishmen, mainly through centuries by Hutton and Evans, had put themselves 300 runs ahead, Mankad played one of the most glorious innings ever seen at Lord's. His hitting was free, swift and vigorous, and roused the spectators to a higher pitch of enthusiasm than had the excellent English batting. He flogged the bowlers until they were tired and then finally, with his score at 184, he was tired himself. His bowling, which, to the spectator's eye, looked almost too easy, was in this match almost as remarkable as his batting. In both innings he bowled ninety-seven overs, of which more than a third were maidens. In the other Tests in which he played it seemed as if he was reckless and got out too easily. But the splendour of his innings at Lord's will be remembered by all who saw it for many a long day. One of the most charming pictures that ever appeared in Wisden is that of Her Majesty the Queen shaking hands with Vinoo Mankad on that glorious day.

7

Pakistan is the newest arrival on the Test match level, and what the 1954 programme will bring forth nobody yet knows. What is certain is that at a meeting of the Imperial Cricket Conference at Lord's on 28th July 1952 Pakistan were admitted to membership of the Conference on the proposition of India, seconded by M.C.C. This seems a beautiful example of Commonwealth co-operation. The other certain fact is that when the M.C.C. touring side of 1951–52 played in Pakistan they found the opposition much stronger than they had expected. Their match at Lahore was drawn, but at Karachi they were defeated on a ground divided, like a Neapolitan ice, into three parts—a matting wicket, a grassy in-field and an out-field of hard-baked mud. After a fairly even game, in which none of the English batsmen, except Tom Graveney, did themselves justice, it came about that A. H. Kardar and a young fellow called Anwar Hussain pulled the game round and brought Pakistan to a win by four wickets. At the end of the game the crowd swept over the ground and garlanded the victors.

Visiting players think that the most interesting Pakistani

player is Hanif Mohammed, an eighteen-year-old schoolboy, who is an opening batsman and also an excellent wicket-keeper. He is a difficult batsman to get rid of, and both English and Indian bowlers have been glad to see the back of him.

The Pakistan player best known to English spectators is undoubtedly A. H. Kardar, who has played (in that order) for Punjab University, India, Oxford University, Warwickshire and Pakistan. The only career as varied as this is that of the famous Sammy Woods, who played for Australia, Cambridge University, Somerset and, on a South African tour, England.

Playing for India in their 1946 tour under the name of Abdul Hafeez, he caused no excitement, a hard-hit 43 in the first Test at Lord's being his only achievement. But at Oxford he was a valuable member of the eleven for the three years 1947–49, both as a forcing left-hand bat and a deceptive spin bowler who could on occasion cause a sudden collapse. In each of his three Varsity matches he batted and bowled well, and when, after going down, he played for a time for Warwickshire, he was always a lively member of a lively side. What he and his friends from Pakistan will do in the summer of 1954 is on the knees of the gods, but it is at least permissible to send birthday greetings to the youngest member of the Commonwealth cricket family.

If I have selected for a profile one player from each of these Commonwealth lands, it is not necessarily because he is the most dazzling cricketer his country has ever produced, but because in some way he is typical, bringing with him the air and colour of his own shores. Member nations of the Commonwealth do not lose anything of their individuality through being bound together by a common sense of values and ideals. And to this English game with its complicated rules these men from sunnier climes can give of their best and lose nothing.

CHAPTER XI

CRICKET MY MISERY

I

I HAVE said it before and will, no doubt, often say it again: cricket is like true love; it has moments of bliss but is mostly agony. The moments of bliss are obvious: the sweet feel of the four struck with the middle of the bat; the rattle of stumps as you deceive the other side's most dangerous batsman; the clean, sharp smack on the palm as you fling out an instinctive hand and the ball miraculously sticks. There are pleasures for the spectator in watching the great ones: a flawless century by Hutton, a bowling performance of courage and penetration by Bedser; an afternoon of Godfrey Evans behind the stumps which some skilled choreographer might have written for him.

There are equal, or almost equal, pleasures for the listener who falls under the spell of a particular broadcast commentator. I learned my listening, if that is the right phrase, ' under ' Howard Marshall, who would describe an innings by Hammond as though it were a regal occasion, as indeed it was. There is great pleasure to be derived from the technical excellences of the modern commentators. The cricket commentator, like any other artist, has to blend skill and feeling. (We all know the musician who is all soul but has no technique, or has tons of technique and no feeling.) I have heard commentators who are statistically unexceptionable but make cricket sound less interesting than noughts and crosses; I have also heard commentators who became highly lyrical but forgot to tell you the score. Among the present commentators there is a rich variety of both knowledge and interest: if I have a favourite in John Arlott it is because he seems to have in his voice an extra shade of human warmth. There is in it a half-humorous, half-affectionate appreciation of cricket as an unending scroll of comedy and character.

These are some of the pleasures; the agonies are equally obvious. There is the agony of the brief encounter when you are bowled first ball; when you miss a man before he has scored and then watch him make a century; when you run yourself out or, worse still, run out the best man on your side— once your friend. When you are a spectator, there is the agony of disaster to the beloved. I once saw my own county beaten by one run. I once drove to Old Trafford to see Maurice Leyland complete a century against the ancient enemy. He was 98 not out. In the first and only over that I saw, Leyland was out leg-before wicket, then came the rain, that punishing local rain which looks as if it would go on for a fortnight. That was the end of play for the day. On the way home I had a puncture and had to push the car half a mile to the nearest garage.

Worst of all is the anguish of winter listening to whatever tribulations an England team may be suffering in Australia or the West Indies. Every time you turn on the radio there is a lowering of morale. While the M.C.C. was last touring in Australia some of the broadcasting was positively macabre. I still shudder to think of it. After crawling out of bed at seven a.m. on a freezing morning, you break the icicles on the loud-speaker and switch on. For the first five minutes you hear nothing but a sound like bath-water gurgling out through a waste-pipe. Then suddenly a cheerful voice says: " Good morning, England. It's a lovely day here. Bailey has just broken his thumb."

And then, think of that first Test match in Jamaica last winter. . . .

Cricket my happiness, indeed!

2

Nobody can conceive the misery I underwent last summer before the Ashes were safe. During the Lord's Test I gave up cricket; not merely playing cricket, but watching, listening to, arguing about and agonizing over cricket. The time was 6.30 p.m. on Monday, 29th June, 1953. I had just seen

England go in to start the task of making 343 in the fourth
innings on a worn pitch.   The hideously incredible score was
20 for three and the victims were Hutton, the Old Master,
Graveney, the Young Master, and Kenyon, the only man who
had scored a century for a county against the Australians that
season.   I could bear no more.   Why should I be lacerated by
raging, tearing emotion?   Even Hamlet, Lear and our other
leading sufferers were never asked to sup on horror to that
extent.   I had devoted far too much of my life to this utterly
irrational game.   I would chuck the whole thing and take to
Strindberg for amusement.

Why, after all that, I should find myself next morning in
St. John's Wood Road is a question for a psychiatrist, and I
would not believe a word a psychiatrist said, anyhow.   It may
have been the criminal returning to the scene of the crime.
It may have been an exceptionally morbid streak in my nature.
At any rate, I found myself in my usual place in front of the
Tavern and there, beside me, was Albert Osmotherly.   Albert
is one of the too many Yorkshiremen who infest Lord's.   He
glared at me:

" Thought you were never coming back? "

" I thought *you* weren't."

He shrugged his shoulders, frowned across at the Father Time
scoreboard—20—3—2—and delivered judgment.

" They'll never get them," he said.

This was an understatement of the position.   All the morning
papers had said, in varying tones of pomposity, recrimination
and disdain, that England would never get them.   It was, they
said, the fault of the weather, the captain, the selectors, the
Minister of Education and the worn patch at the Nursery End.

" What's more," said Albert, " they don't deserve to win."

" Why not, if they could? "

" Hutton," he asserted accusingly, " dropped three catches."

" What of it? " I retorted, stung momentarily out of my
coma.   " Nelson was often sea-sick."

Albert plunged back into gloom.

The umpires came out.   The fieldsmen came out.   The

batsmen, Compton and Watson, came out. It seemed almost
strange that a clergyman did not meet them at the pavilion
gate.

" I'll give 'em till lunch time," said Albert as though he were
making a wildly generous offer.

From the beginning play was quiet, with all the pensive
tranquillity of obsequies at which the hearse has not yet
turned up. Suddenly Compton forgot he was at a funeral and
hit three fours. When I clapped, Albert looked at me dis-
approvingly.

" Oh, him," said Albert. He said this with no personal
disrespect but from a firm conviction that southerners were not
serious characters. And by a southerner he meant, of course, a
man born south of a line drawn between Sheffield and Barnsley.

At twenty to one Compton was out for a polished 33 and
Bailey came in.

" Oh, him," said Albert.

At lunch the score, against all probabilities, was 114 for 4.

" At least," I said, " they've lasted till now."

" You wait," muttered Albert, as though he had a couple of
earthquakes up his sleeve.

I do not know what time hope began to revive, like a numbed
gum coming out of a local anaesthetic. Slowly it dawned on
me that, come rope, come rack, seven men still lived with bats
in their hands. Why should not at least some of them survive?
Albert looked shocked when I put this to him.

" You must be daft," he said.

There was something almost uncanny in the way Watson and
Bailey supported my daftness. Watson, fair, trim and cool,
took the good balls in the middle of the bat and pulled the short
ones, with force and velocity, away to leg. Bailey, with con-
sistent courage, got in the way of the ball, mostly with the bat,
sometimes with the pad and sometimes, painfully, with the
fingers. But if he observed subconsciously: " This hurts me
more than it hurts you," it gave the bowlers no comfort. The
bowlers toiled and spun, Lindwall with controlled fury, Johnston with force and guile, Miller with windmill whirlings,

Benaud with quickish tweakers and Ring with waspish cunning.
Yet in vain. Were these the avenging furies that had torn
England to tatters the evening before? When Watson and
Bailey went in for tea at 183 for four, I would willingly have
subscribed to a fund for providing both of them with gold cups
and platinum saucers.

" You wait," said Albert. " Tea always unsettles them."

It was over an hour after tea before anything unsettled them.
Ball by ball, confidence grew, not in the hearts of Watson and
Bailey, who had had supreme confidence all along, but in the
spectators, who began to gather flickering hope. And hope
naturally bred anxiety. As hope gleamed, terrors revived.
The crowd showed a slight tendency to gasp and groan, and to
sigh with relief when the ball was safe, untouched, in the
wicket-keeper's gloves. I died a thousand deaths and would
not have missed one of them.

It was at ten to six, when the heroic pair looked as though
they would remain for ever in their heroic attitudes that
Watson suddenly became mortal, touched one to the slips and
then, as fate so often wills, his partner departed soon after.
The match was back in the melting-pot and hearts were in
mouths again. Were we fair to Freddy Brown, who, though
grand, is grandly fallible? The more he made us nervous with
his bold and ponderous hits, the more we cheered him, and
Evans too, though he was not quite getting the ball in the middle
of the bat as he gets them in the middle of his gloves. Ten past
six, quarter past six, twenty past, twenty-five past. . . . I shut
my eyes. Brown was out. All round me people were frenziedly
counting how many balls there were to come. Johnny Wardle
came along. If he had a care in the world, it did not show.
One, two, three. Wardle, a born survivor, survived. The
umpires took off the bails. Who dies, if England lives? The
crowd went mad. Albert flung his hat in the air and leaped
to meet it in the first steps of a wild Zulu war-dance.

" I knew they'd do it," he panted, " but it doesn't do to
speak too soon."

3

And if I suffered at Lord's, what of Headingley? Do you remember a film in which Naunton Wayne and the ever-lamented Basil Radford wandered round Europe, worrying in a delightfully ridiculous way about what was happening in the Test match at Manchester? Like so many misfortunes that occur to other folk, it seemed funny at the time. I waited until the Manchester Test was safely over. (If I didn't have a heart attack when Australia finished at 35 for eight, I shall live to be a hundred.) That should have been good enough. Before the 1953 Leeds Test came along I was determined to stand no nonsense. I was going to visit romantic Austria and moonlit Venice, Bride of the Adriatic. Surely, after Wardle had taken four for 7, a man might be allowed to relax for a fortnight. What a fellow wants is to get away from the atom bomb, the cold war and the imminence of national bankruptcy; in short, all the dull routine of everyday life, and soak his soul in peace and beauty. Though, of course, it was difficult for the soul to be at rest, with Hutton suffering from fibrositis. . . .

I deliberately turned my back on my own country. All went well at first. The sea was calm, the journey across Belgium and Germany was full of interest, and there was pleasure, not to mention instruction, in seeing Turin, Milan and the long cause-way that leads to Venice. . . . That first glimpse in the soft evening light of the Grand Canal has an enchantment that age cannot wither. Byron saw it. The Brownings saw it. The passenger in the gondola abreast of mine saw it, leaned forward in wonder at it and, as he did so, accidentally dropped his hat in the water.

He said, unexpectedly and rather loudly, that it was a fair cow, and this peculiar ejaculation rather than any marked accent, stamped him as a citizen of the great Australian Commonwealth. When I retrieved his hat for him, we discovered that we were being paddled to the same hotel. He was an amiable companion and our relations from the beginning were extremely pleasant. I was determined not to be the first to

mention the Test match.   He talked to me of mediæval glass,
the magic of San Marco and Ruskin's *Stones of Venice.*   I talked
to him about Bondi Beach, Chips Rafferty and the ornitho-
rhyncus or duck-billed water-mole.   I hope I appeared witty
and nonchalant.   It was hard work.

   " Never mind," I said to myself, " I'll find an English paper
tomorrow."

   But I was unlucky.   The following day I searched Venice
from the Bridge of Sighs to the Lido (pavilion end), without
even finding out whether England had lost the toss.   (I need
not have worried about that.   Hutton never won the toss that
year.)   My Australian friend, whose name was Martin, kept
slipping away on the pretext of posting post-cards or buying
some Venetian glass to send to his wife, but he always came
back without (I suspected) having found what he wanted.
Before he left Venice he was beginning to have a haggard look.
I had, I think, lost several pounds myself.

   We came back from Italy to Austria by coach over the
historic Brenner Pass.   The majestic Dolomites were wreathed
in clouds, and Martin and I were wrapped in silence.   It was
in the Customs shed at the frontier that I first saw an English
newspaper.   It was stuffed under the straps of a rucksack
worn by a big bony citizen in the crowd in front of me.   I had
virtually to stand on my head to see it and what I saw played
havoc with my blood-pressure.

   " Feeling faint? " asked Martin considerately.

   " If I can read upside down," I murmured, " Hutton has got
a duck."

   " Ha-ha—I mean, sorry.   You'd better have a stiff peg of
slivowitz.   That should pull you round."

   For the next four days my agony was less in extent but more
concentrated.   Hampered though we were by the ignorance of
foreigners, we managed to ascertain the score once, or nearly
once, a day.   We had to fight for every paper, just as England
was fighting for every run.   In Innsbruck I followed a respectable old gentleman the length of the famous Maria-Theresien-
strasse under the impression that he was carrying the *Man-*

chester Guardian, only to discover that he was really a German professor, flourishing the *Frankfurter Zeitung*.

(England 167, Australia 161 for three.) At the moment when we obtained the news, from a kindly American who little knew how he was turning the dagger in my wound, that Australia had filched—you couldn't call it scored—48 for the last wicket, we were standing in front of the great cathedral at Salzburg, listening to Mozart, a man whom, in my less agitated moments, I have always considered as good as Victor Trumper in his own line. We were actually hanging by a bit of wire in the hair-raising cable railway car 5,000 feet above the Hungerburg plateau, like peas in a matchbox, when we learned, from a sympathetic fellow-pea, that England's fate hung equally in the balance. Hutton was out in the second innings, too, but Edrich and Compton, old campaigners both, were making a fight of it. But we never heard another word that day.

It was on the way home that Fate began to turn the screw. We set off on a long railway journey, through a corner of Germany, back into Austria, and then into Germany again. Leaving the train we boarded a steamer, like a Mississippi show-boat, to sail between castled crags and vine-clad slopes along the poet's ' wide and winding Rhine '. It was while passing the notorious Lorelei rock that I learned that five English batsmen had been lured to their doom and that my beloved country was only about 70 runs on. Why did I ever leave home? I should never have strayed all this way from Headingley, much less from my own wireless set.

After that we were on the long night train. I do not suppose Martin slept well. I know I did not. The train roared through the darkness. It was three o'clock before I dozed off. When I woke we were at Cologne. I stumbled out sleepily on to a darkened platform By some miracle there was a bookstall right in front of me and, what was more, an English paper. I flung the boy a mark (about one and eightpence) and bundled back into the train. What was this? There was only one event in contemporary English history which interested me, and I could find no mention of it, Our return journey had brought us in front of schedule. This was Thursday's paper. I had missed the result, which would have been published in Wednesday's. In quiet despair I tumbled asleep.

When the train stopped next, it was at Aix-la-Chapelle; now it was Martin's turn to forage for a newspaper. I watched him toddle down the windy platform, a flapping overcoat over his pyjamas. I watched him as he located the paper-trolley. He laid his hand on the newspaper, but, before he could open it, a frolic wind snatched it from his grasp and whisked it, provokingly, exasperatingly, maddeningly along the tracks. As he dashed after it in frenzied pursuit, our train moved off, quietly but inexorably, towards Ostend. I suppose a draw was a fair result.

And, of course, we did win at the Oval. I never saw Martin again. Such a nice fellow.

CHAPTER XII

WINTER MADE GLORIOUS

I

WINTER in England is a time of raw, foggy days, of running colds and streaming umbrellas, when a man has practically no friends in the world but his goloshes, and when he has nothing more to look forward to at the end of the day but one small whisky, two large aspirins, and a lukewarm hot-water bottle. That is England in winter, and never were time and place more entitled to separation on grounds of incompatibility.

Would it not be wonderful if, by the stretching of a finger, by the mere turning of a vulcanite knob, you could be transported from the murk and the mud of the city streets to a land of cloudless turquoise skies, emerald-green velvet turf and clear air dancing and shimmering in the heat haze? Wonderful, perhaps, but not impossible. Turn on the radio and listen. If you listen at the right time, you will discover that cricket will be going on in one of many sunny climes and a welcome voice will be telling you about it. You may not always like what he tells you. The facts may be grim for England. But the facts of life are grim, anyhow. That is not the point.

The voice could conceivably come from Brisbane, Bombay, Barbados, or from any one of a score of blessed plots in Australia, South Africa, India, New Zealand or the West Indies. (Whatever evil tidings may have come from Sabina Park, Kingston, Jamaica, it will still be an enchanted ground under the shade of green palm and blue mountain.) These places lie in the happier southern hemisphere; all, that is, except India and the West Indies, which are near enough to the equator for hemispheres not to matter. Blue sky, golden sun, green turf; all this and cricketers' heaven, too, except that in some places the ground is not green but brown and the pitch is a tightly stretched matting. As if that made any difference, except to the naughtier bowlers. . . .

Long before the birth of radio and, solemn thought, of its attendant Arlotts and Alstons, cricket under a less wintry sun lived and had its being and men went out from England to do battle under fairer skies than those that hang over Lord's in winter or Old Trafford in summer. All good things must have a beginning, and the first Test match, the very first Test that ever was, took place at Melbourne in 1877. To be fair the month was March and the English winter should have been nearly over, but the records tell us that it was a bad year and gentlemen in England then abed must have snuggled down tightly under the blankets while they thought that somebody or something was warm, 12,000 miles away.

The Australian side on that day in 1877 contained a few names that you will naturally remember. Charles Bannerman, elder brother of the other Bannerman (Alec) who stonewalled his way through five tours in this country; Midwinter, who afterwards came to England and played for Gloucester; D. W. Gregory, first of a whole gaggle of Gregorys; and the stumper J. M. Blackham, owner of cricket's fiercest beard (always excepting W. G.'s), the toughest appendage since that of Blackbeard the Buccaneer. The English team contained names which are still freshly remembered, at least in the north country; five of them were Yorkshiremen: Happy Jack Ulyett and Tom Emmett, the two most famous of the old Yorkshire players; Allan Hill and Andrew Greenwood, who came, you will remember, from Lascelles Hall; and Tom Armitage, the stout fellow who, in the New Zealand floods, had carried the lady across the river on his back. The captain was James Lillywhite, Junior, the Sussex pro., which shows that Len Hutton was not his country's first professional captain. Besides Lillywhite and his five Yorkshiremen there was Harry Jupp, the Surrey batsman who had to keep wicket because Ted Pooley had been left behind in New Zealand, and Alfred Shaw, the renowned Notts slow bowler. Somebody had to bowl the first ball in any Test, and this honour fell to Alfred himself, for whom it was claimed that he never bowled a wide or a no-ball all his life. Bannerman hit the first run; he also hit 164 more. Somebody is said to have missed him before he scored, but why should I tell you who it was? Historians are now giving even Richard III the benefit of the doubt. The bowlers could not get Bannerman out, though his partners fell regularly by the wayside, until a nasty breakback ball from Ulyett suddenly rose and hit him on the hand. Into retirement he had to go. . . .

Bannerman's score amounted to two-thirds of the whole and the crowd collected 165 sovereigns, one for each run. When England went in, they never quite caught up. Jupp scored the first half-century ever made for England, but nobody else produced any fireworks until Allan Hill, the handsome fellow from Lascelles Hall, carried his bat for a truculently hammered 35.

In the second innings the English bowlers were too much for the Australians and nobody could make anything of Alfred Shaw and Ulyett. Bannerman, his hand in bandages, scored only one run. When England went in to get 154, which did not seem too difficult, they fared just as badly. Kendall took seven for 55, and a swashbuckling 38 from Ulyett was the best contribution to an inadequate English total of 108. So Australia won the first Test match and that is how it all started.

The first Test in South Africa was played in our winter of 1888–89, also a winter of rough weather. Playing on the charming ground at Port Elizabeth, the English team was hardly formidable as an international side, but it was never-theless too strong for an infant South Africa, and who do you think was the English captain? A tall, slim undergraduate named C. A. ('Round the Corner') Smith, who was named partly after his bowling action and partly after a character in Surtees. C. A. Smith lived another sixty years, achieved a well-deserved knighthood, and (solemn thought) taught Hollywood cricket and court etiquette, in that order. He took five wickets for 19 in the South Africans' first innings, and they simply did not know which corner he was bowling round. England won by eight wickets, although nobody but Bobby Abel made a respectable score. A fortnight later there was another Test, also on a very pleasant ground, at Capetown. Abel made his usual century, but England's innings victory was due not so much to this as to the slightly fantastic bowling of Johnny Briggs, who in the two innings took fifteen wickets for 28 runs. Repeat: fifteen for 28. And fourteen of them were clean bowled. There can never have been such hitting of the stumps before or since, even by Schofield Haigh.

What of those other English winters? It was in the same period—1929–30—that the first away Tests were played not only against the West Indies, but also against New Zealand. On the 11th January to 16th January, 1930, an English eleven under the Hon. F. S. G. Calthorpe played the West Indies on the lovely Barbados ground at Kensington Oval—I said *Kensington*. There was some tall scoring by Sandham for England and, for the West Indies, by Roach and George Headley of the panther-like spring, who made the first of his many centuries. (At the age of forty-four he was brought back to the West Indies by public subscription to take part in the 1953–54 Tests against England.) This was Constantine's first Test at home, though he had, of course, visited England the previous summer and achieved ' the double '. In the West Indies his batting and bowling for once fell short of the spectacular, but he made four of those incredible catches by which the quickness of his hands perennially deceived the eye.

In New Zealand, at Lancaster Park, Christchurch, an English eleven, which included Woolley and Duleepsinhji, got seven New Zealand wickets down for 21 runs, mainly through some sensational bowling by M. J. C. Allom, who laid the foundations of a fairly easy victory for his side by taking four wickets in five balls.

The first Test played in India began at Bombay four years later and saw centuries by B. H. Valentine on one side and L. Amarnath on the other. There was also some fine attacking bowling by Maurice Nichols and Mohamed Nissar. In the end

England won without great difficulty by nine wickets, but it was the beginning of a shining period which gave English cricket-lovers the pleasures that came from playing against or watching Merchant, Mankad, Hazare and Umrigar.

If I were asked to think of a match which, beyond many others, truly made winter glorious, I would recall Bobby Peel's match at Sydney in December 1894. I did not see it, because it took place round about the time I was born, but there are times when I have *felt* that match, just as I have *seen* the 1893 York-shire *v.* Lancashire match through the eager eyes of Uncle Walter. At Sydney England faced the mountainous task of following on against an Australian total of 586, and it is to their credit that they fought back with tenacity. The first hero was Albert Ward, the man whom Uncle Walter saw catch Ulyett off the last ball of that Lancashire *v.* Yorkshire game. Ward made 100 and there were several forties; even so, Australia were set only 177 to win, and they started off with cheerful confidence. On the evening of the fifth day they were 113 with only two wickets down. It was in the bag. There was a clattering thunderstorm during the night, and when Bobby Peel and Johnny Briggs went down to Sydney Oval in the morning to look at the wicket, the sun was shining fiercely. Bobby dug his toe into the turf and exclaimed with gleeful wickedness: " That's for me ! " The third wicket fell at 130 and the whole of the rest of the Australian team put on only 36 more. Five of the last six wickets fell to Peel, and England, after following on 261 behind, had won by 10 runs.

> Now is the winter of our discontent
> Made glorious summer by this sun of York . . .

At any rate, I think the sons of Yorkshire have done their share.

2

Cricket makes winter, if not glorious, at least bearable. Even such shattering news as we heard from the West Indies last January, though unhappy, did not cast any Eng-land supporter permanently down. Defeat should be borne philosophically, but not too philosophically.   It is no philosophy not to *dislike* defeat.   It is not true philosophy, either, to dwell nostalgically on the glories of the past, without attempting to eradicate the faults of the present.   That does not mean that the past should be neglected.   If I admire the best of the past, it is not for the purpose of disdaining the present, but to underline the continuity of history.

Some of the old players had the right way of looking at the matter.   They had enjoyment, zest and an instinctive sense of playing to finish a game and win it.   If they won, they were happy.   If they lost, like the twenty thousand Cornishmen of the song, they would know the reason why.   One reason for their success was that they were continuously and exuberantly themselves.   Happy Jack Ulyett and Tom Emmett undoubtedly were.   Here was self-expression in its only intelligible sense.   Of Tom, the great Richard Daft said that he was all wire and whipcord, the best stuff a cricketer was ever made of.

Old Arthur Fielder, who died in 1947, shook his head in good-humoured scorn over some of the younger generation whom he considered to be too pampered.

" Too much mollycoddling, too many sweaters, not enough beef and too weak beer."

It may be that some of the younger lads are less urgent in effort than they might be.   It is well known that Bradman when young would practise throwing the ball at a narrow rounded rail.   This task was self-imposed and, if he missed the rail, he had to field the ball a long, long way.   And George Hirst told me recently: " When I was a lad at Kirkheaton, we took the side nets away and every ball had to be fielded."

Batsmen who complain to-day of an occasional bumper might draw comfort from the thought that when the ball left Alfred Mynn's bowling hand, it audibly hummed; or from the contemplation of the menacing figure of Sammy Woods, who on coming on to bowl, would courteously inquire of his victim: " Where will you 'ave it?   On the 'ead or the 'eart? "

There are few discouragements of the present which have not at some time had their counterparts in the past.   The infrequent bumpers sent down by Miller or Trueman are mild offerings compared with those sent down in the days when 'Jackson's pace was very fearful', when pitches were rougher and umpires were perhaps less humane than now. In the days when the famous Barlow—O my Barlow!—kept a sports equipment shop in his home town he was once greeted by a long-faced customer who inquired lugubriously:

"Do you keep sporting necessaries?"

"Yes, sir."

"Then put me up a bottle of arnica, a roll of court-plaster, and a sling for my arm. I'm playing against Crossland this afternoon."

It was the notorious Jackson of the fearful pace who admitted that he had never taken all ten wickets in an innings. "But," he added in a mood of sentimental reminiscence, "I once got nine and lamed Johnny Wisden."

Complaints are sometimes heard about the quality of present-day umpiring, especially in countries of the Commonwealth other than our own. I am certain that if errors are made they do not arise through ill-will, but through lack of the widest experience. If we compare the size of the season's programme in India, the West Indies or even Australia with the (perhaps excessive) first-class programme in England, the inequality of opportunities is plain. To demand neutral umpires is foolish: all umpires are neutral in intention; what a few of them need is not more impartiality, but more practice.

But the eccentricities of umpires, at all but the highest levels, have always been, and especially in the old days, a matter for occasional tragedy and frequent comedy. The old country umpire was ever a fellow-citizen of Dogberry and Verges. You will find few now of the calibre of the ancient type who would say: "Lunch and tea-time That's what umpires think on most." Nor will you find many of the home-based variety who were there loyally to support their friends and would meet all appeals from visiting bowlers with an obdurate: "Not out, not out, and I bet you half a crown we win!"

There was a famous old umpire of Boroughbridge in Yorkshire

who found himself in a difficulty when, in the last over of the game, his own side needed four runs to win. The bowler bowled and the umpire called: " No ball." The bowler bowled again and again the umpire called: " No ball." The third ball was a beauty that just shaved the stumps, but still the umpire repeated his cry of " No ball." The bowler, visibly rattled, sent down a long hop which the batsman promptly hit for four and the match was won. As the umpire left the middle he called out to the home side's scorer: " Hey, Charlie, rub them no balls out. We don't need 'em! "

Alec Watson, the old Scottish slow bowler who carried Lancashire a long way in his time, used to say: " What, me take up umpiring? Not as long as I can see twenty-two yards. . . ." No wonder. . . .

In my own modest type of village game I always found the ideas of some players odder than those of the umpires. I remember once mildly querying the propriety of appealing for a leg-before-wicket decision from the square-leg position. (This was when I was very young. I should hardly, in this day and age, query the propriety of *anything*.)

" Why not? " demanded the fieldsman. " My mate, the bowler, he appeals for direction, and I appeals for height! "

I remember, too, a reluctantly departing batsman requiring to know who had altered the rule which caused him to be given out leg-before-wicket to an off-break ball.

" The M.C.C.," was the reply.

" And what the hell," he demanded, " has it got to do with them? "

I should say that the modern first-class umpire, who rightly treats his job as a technical subject, is more competent than his predecessors; even Bob Thoms, or Jim Phillips, who always carried a Hall and Knight's *Algebra* in his pocket. Phillips, who, you will remember, no-balled Ernest Jones in Australia, came to England and played for Middlesex as a stock bowler. After that he became an umpire and took the unpopular but probably correct decision to no-ball Arthur Mold, the Lancashire fast bowler, for throwing. But the strangest thing that happened to Phillips occurred when he no-balled C. B. Fry in a Sussex *v.* Oxford University match. In the second innings Fry came out with his fore-arm in a splint, but his captain would not put him on.

The umpires of the old days were honest and keen, but probably had fewer complications to deal with than the present ones. There were probably never better umpires in any age than Frank Chester and Dai Davies.

The umpiring story I like best is of the old lion, Fuller Pilch, umpiring in his later years, and scarcely concealing his scorn for what he conceived to be the game's decline and fall from his own great days. When bowlers appealed for leg-before-wicket, he would growl:

" Come on, bowl 'em out, *bowl* 'em out! "

3

I suppose cricketers to-day differ from their grandfathers in much the same way as the times themselves differ. General conditions have changed, and the particular conditions of the player's life have greatly improved since the time of Pooley and Pinder. Wages are better and there is a better chance of security. Rightly so. The bigger benefits are bigger still, though I would rather have had the worth of George Hirst's £3,703 in 1904 than some of the modern benefits which are three times as large on paper. It is a commonplace to say that while cricket has a perhaps generally higher level, there are few outstanding figures. Of this I would say that it is not true or, alternatively, that it is comparatively true at the present day in all walks of life. I cannot think Hutton, Bedser and Evans would not have been outstanding cricketers (and men) in any age. On the other hand, when the level of the tableland is raised, there are bound to be fewer peaks. So the average young cricketer, just like any other youngster whom you meet to-day, tends to be like his fellows: modest, well-mannered, fairly skilled in a technical way, a little sophisticated, but not remarkable in individual character. They are certainly not relentless in resolve and concentration, as were, say, Bradman and Sutcliffe, to go no further back Always apart from Hutton, whose fine concentration is a thing apart, few moderns have this resolution. One who undoubtedly has it is Trevor Bailey, whose determination in recent Tests is beyond praise. Another, just as undoubtedly, is Stuart Surridge, captain of Surrey, the first by-product of whose boldness of temper has been Surrey's emergence as champion county twice—and why not thrice?—in succession. As a Yorkshireman I am not enamoured of the idea of Surrey as permanent champions, but if Surrey achieve their victories in the spirit, and by the methods, of the old triumphant Yorkshire, what am I to say? On two counts, Surridge is a great captain. I remember C. B. Fry being asked : " They say you were a great captain ; is that so ? " And he replied : " Of course. I had great bowlers." Surridge has England's two best bowlers, in addition to himself, and this automatically makes the best bowling side in the country. As for leadership, it is there by inspiration and example and by sheer vitality in the field, which is one of the most urgent spurs a side can have. Catches seem to go to him as smaller fish go into the mouth of a giant pike. And his legitimate hostility on the field is only exceeded by his broad friendliness off.

But what I miss among my younger friends is that sheer ' chunkiness ' of the older players whose characters seemed to be cast in a more solid and rounded mould. For instance, you may to-day read highly scientific books or articles on the technique of bowling, but will never discover the heart of the matter as it was revealed by Mr. David Buchanan, a Scot who settled in England and played for the Gentlemen in the 'sixties, 'seventies and 'eighties. A fast bowler who had turned into a very successful slow one, he would say : " The ball ought not to come from the bowler's hand like a lump of lead. It ought to come as if it had a fiend inside it, which works the mischief immediately it touches the ground."

I like the spirit of attack in Tom Emmett's observation to his colleague, Allan Hill of Lascelles Hall, Yorkshire and England : " Come on, Allan, thee *flay* [1] 'em out and I'll bowl 'em out ! "

---

[1] Frighten.

I cannot think of anyone of whom it could be said as old Bob Carpenter said of W. G.: " It's worse to be with him than against him. When you were fielding there might be an odd ball that you didn't have to run for, but if you were batting with him, never! "

Sometimes there was the sharp irony that lies deep in English character. When James Shaw missed W. G. off an easy return catch, he did not dance with rage, as we have seen Tom Emmett do. Instead, he shrugged his shoulders and murmured: " Ah, well, I like to see him bat."

Have we anybody of the nonchalance of that mighty hitter C. I. (' Buns ') Thornton, famous for wrecking, if not the roofs of distant towns, at least the windows of nearby houses, particularly outside the Scarborough ground? One day, he broke a window twice with successive balls, and when the owner complained, Thornton replied thoughtfully: " Well, perhaps you'd better leave it open. . . ."

It was Thornton who gave what was perhaps the first and last dictum on cricket eugenics. When Bonnor, the Australian hitter, said to Thornton in humorous scorn: " I've got a sister back home who can hit as well as you! ", he replied: " Right, bring her over and we'll marry her to Louis Hall! "

I like to think of the Hon. C. J. Lyttelton, whose father used to come to Lord's to watch him bat, but would read a copy of *Herodotus* all the rest of the time.

Of those happy survivors from the old-time cricket to the new I would name Sir Pelham Warner, Ashes-winning captain of 1903–04, and said by many fine cricketers, including Patsy Hendren, to be the best captain they have ever served under. When he first played, W. G. Grace was still captaining the Gentlemen; when he retired in 1920 his county had gloriously won the championship. And never during all that time did his unfailing courtesy mitigate his unfailing keenness. That year did not by any means see the end of his career; it merely saw a continuance of his service to the game and its followers, as a selector, administrator, and elder statesman. I doubt if any man of any age has ever given the game more unselfish, devoted service.   There is a story of his taking with some friends a short holiday in the South of France, though I do not know how he tore himself away from Lord's, even for a day or two.   While admiring the beauties, sacred and architectural, of a charming little church, suddenly he turned and purposefully walked down the full length of the nave.   A happy smile spread over his features: "Just as I thought," he murmured, " twenty-two yards exactly."

On his eightieth birthday his friends gave him a dinner in the Long Room at Lord's from where, through the winter darkness, he could see the scoreboard illuminated with the legend 80 *NOT OUT*.   In his lively and gracious person, as in those of my friends, C. B. Fry and George Hirst, the game is visibly carried through from the old good days to the present good days.   So may it ever be.

Cricket is a microcosm of the land that gave it birth; it has the English traditions of freedom within the law and of respect for individual character and skilled craftsmanship.   Even geographically it follows a historic pattern, so that to the national whole the regions have made, and can make, their own contributions of northern grit, of western vitality and southern culture and elegance.   Yorkshire and Lancashire, Gloucester and Somerset, Sussex and Kent: have not these counties given to cricket something symbolic of what they have given to the larger field of England's history?   A Leyland, a Hammond, a Woolley: these are men who flourished the banner of their own county and gave England what England most needed in their time.

If a man wanted to see England, he might do worse than tour its cricket-grounds during a not too severe summer; in the villages, in the country towns, in the counties, both urban and rural.   He will find the country grounds in some of the loveliest settings in the land; as for the town grounds, he will come upon them as welcome oases in deserts of brick and mortar.   He will find the players keen, skilled and even-tempered; he will find the spectators penetrating, knowledgeable and frankly partisan, though not partisan beyond reason.

There will he find no enemy. Indeed, he will find an England masculine, cultivated and even-minded; and as nearly merry as any country has any need or right to be.

While cricket flourishes, England is not doing too badly. It is not necessarily prosperous, not necessarily free from trouble, but it is likely to be confident and serene; likely to be united and sure enough in its own way of life to be tolerant and happy. Very well, then. Come the four corners of the world in arms, and we will. . . . Now I come to think of it, we have not the slightest desire to shock them. But we will give them a good game.

INDEX